THE KISTE AND OGAN SOCIAL CHANGE

SERIES IN ANTHROPOLOGY

Editors

ROBERT C. KISTE   EUGENE OGAN

University of Minnesota

David Jacobson was born in New Jersey where he spent his early school years. He was awarded a Ph.D. in 1967 at the University of Rochester. In 1965 and 1966 Dr. Jacobson was a Research Associate with the East African Institute of Social Research (Uganda).

An appointment at the University of Connecticut, as an assistant professor, was followed by a move to Brandeis University.

His specializations are social anthropology and urban social organization in Africa and the United States. Currently, Dr. Jacobson is heading a study on changing attitudes and adjustment of engineers thrown into unemployment by the recession. He is a member of both the American Anthropological Association and the African Studies Association.

ITINERANT TOWNSMEN

Cummings Publishing Company

Friendship and Social Order in Urban Uganda

DAVID JACOBSON

Brandeis University

Menlo Park, California

Cummings Publishing Company, Inc.
2727 Sand Hill Road
Menlo Park, California 94025

Foreword

Dr. David Jacobson's study is one of the initial volumes in the series of ethnographic case studies on social and cultural change published by Cummings Publishing Company. With the exception of a few small populations in the most remote regions of the earth, no society today remains unaffected by other social groups and the stream of current events. The studies comprising the series reflect this basic state of man's condition in the latter part of the twentieth century, and they focus on a common theme: the ways in which members of contemporary societies respond to and develop strategies to cope with modifications of their social and physical environments.

Each study in the series is based on field research conducted by the author. In addition to focusing his study around the theme of the series, each author is encouraged to develop other relevant theoretical implications of his material. Studies from the major geographical and cultural areas of the world are represented in forthcoming volumes, and the series provides a fairly even balance between literate and non-literate societies. It is hoped that the studies will provide the materials from which some generalizations and conclusions about the processes of social and cultural change may be generated.

I n some respects, the present study represents a departure from some of the traditional orientations of anthropology; to place this study in perspective, a few comments on the history of the discipline are appropriate. For a relatively long period of time, anthropologists concerned themselves with relatively small-scale, traditional societies of the non-Western world. These societies, commonly referred to as primitive or non-literate, were usually less complex in structure than modern nation states.

During anthropology's developmental period in the latter part of the nineteenth century, scholars examined the range of variation in different societies and attempted to discover the origin and development of human culture by the comparative study of diverse societies as described in the accounts of explorers, missionaries, and colonial administrators. After the turn of the century, anthropologists turned to the study of individual societies and cultures with the aim of understanding each as a unique entity with its own cultural patterns and structure. A strong tradition of field research grounded in the technique of participant observation became one of the hallmarks of the anthropological endeavor.

Not until the late 1920's and early 1930's did anthropologists begin to concern themselves with the changes in traditional societies which were occurring as a consequence of their contact with other peoples and nations, mainly those of the West. Over the next two decades, a large number of studies of acculturation and culture-contact situations appeared. Most of the studies focused on changes within traditional societies, ignoring or not taking into full account the fact that those societies were inextricably embedded within the framework of large-scale colonial empires or contemporary nation states.

In more recent years, anthropologists have become increasingly aware that the peoples with whom they have been concerned can be understood only when set in the context of the large societies of which they are a part. As a result, a growing number of researchers have expanded their efforts to include the study of "complex" societies, and they are examining the network of relations which function to incorporate the members of small traditional societies into the larger social structures of nation states and colonial empires. In the vast majority of cases, the peoples who have been the focus of anthropological research occupy subordinate positions in the lower socioeconomic levels of large-scale societies, and their lives and destinies are largely controlled and determined by elite classes possessing power and economic advantage. While this fact is obvious even to the most casual observer, few anthropologists have investigated the cultures and life-styles of those elite classes who have so much influence over the peoples with which they have been long concerned.

Dr. Jacobson's study is an investigation into this neglected area of inquiry and is a contribution both to modern urban anthropology and to the general area of sociocultural change. He traces the development of the town of Mbale, an urban center in modern Uganda, and outlines the division of its people into elite and non-elite social classes. Relations between the two classes are examined, but the focus of the study is upon the life-style, cultural values, and patterns of social interaction among members of the elite who occupy bureaucratic and professional statuses in Ugandan society.

The elite, in this case black Africans, come from diverse tribal backgrounds, and they have a high degree of mobility as they are frequently transferred from one urban locale to another. Jacobson provides a careful examination of the cultural and social processes which function to define the boundaries of the elite class, maintain social order, and provide the basis for networks of social relations which give individuals meaning and security in the otherwise precarious and fluctuating urban environment. Most significantly, Jacobson's analysis challenges the commonly held notion that voluntary associations or corporate groups of some variety are the functional prerequisites for urban life and that the absence of such institutions necessarily results in social disorganization and personal anomie. Dr. Jacobson's comparison of Mbale society with urban populations in other locales in Africa and in the United States provides a number of insights and raises a number of issues which can be resolved only by future research.

While Dr. Jacobson's study is a venture into a novel subject matter, his research techniques are familiar to the anthropologist. Documentary materials are drawn upon for historical background. Data on contemporary Mbale were gathered by the usual anthropological technique of participant observation, and the quality of the study indicates that the technique may be employed as a research strategy as fruitfully in complex urban societies as it has been in traditional ones.

Other series' volumes to be published by Cummings, notably, Frank C. Miller's *Old Villages and a New Town*, probe some of the problems examined in this volume and will be of interest to students of urban life.

<table>
<tr><td>*University of Minnesota*</td><td>ROBERT C. KISTE</td></tr>
<tr><td>*Minneapolis, Minnesota*</td><td>EUGENE OGAN</td></tr>
<tr><td>*June, 1972*</td><td>*Series Editors*</td></tr>
</table>

Acknowledgments

I am indebted to several people and institutes for their support in the preparation of this study. Professor H. Smythe first interested me in the new elite Africans. The National Institute of Mental Health awarded me a research grant (1 RO4 MH 11477-01 BEH), which enabled me to undertake field work. While I was in Uganda, the staff of the East African Institute of Social Research, in particular Professor Josef Gugler, greatly facilitated my research in Mbale. I give special thanks to Professors Alfred Harris and Robert S. Merril, of the University of Rochester, for their part in my graduate training and for the attention they gave to the dissertation from which this present analysis developed. Furthermore, I express my appreciation to the people of Mbale, Africans and non-Africans, elite and non-elite, for having allowed me to learn something about their way of life and for having made my stay in Mbale a pleasant one. Acknowledgment is also due to the editors of *Southwestern Journal of Anthropology*, the *Journal of Asian and African Studies*, and *Man* for permission to include within this study materials published in their journals. Finally, and above all, I thank my wife, Sue, for sharing the field-work experience with me and for her encouragement during the writing of this book. I happily dedicate this book to her.

Waltham, Massachusetts
June, 1972

DAVID JACOBSON

Contents

Illustrations

PHOTOGRAPHS

MAPS

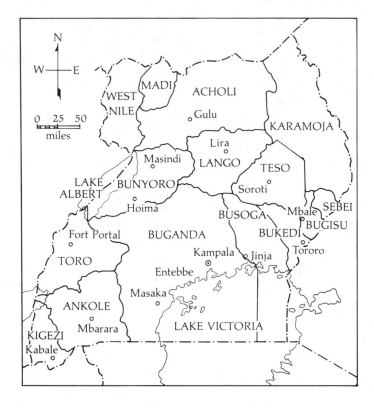

CHAPTER ONE

Map 1. Districts and Urban Centers of Uganda

Introduction

Urbanization has been one of the most dramatic developments in Africa's recent history. Within the past thirty-five
years large numbers of Africans have responded to the political
and economic changes resulting from the colonial experience
by leaving their traditional, rural way of life and flooding into
the cities and towns, both old and new. In East Africa, Uganda's urban centers have been caught up in this process: between 1948 and 1959, the population of its largest city
expanded by almost 60 percent and that of its two major towns
more than doubled, and they have continued to grow since
then. This rate of growth is significant not only for the changes
it has brought about in the rural areas, but also for the new
social conditions and the new patterns of social life it has
produced in the urban centers.

Urban life in Uganda is characterized by populations
which are large, heterogeneous, and geographically mobile.
The number, diversity, and transiency of townsmen generates
anonymity among them, which, in turn, creates uncertainty
and a potential for social disorder. The mobility of the population is particularly significant in this respect; there is frequent
movement of individuals from one place of residence to another within a city or town, from town to town, and from
urban centers to rural areas and back again. Yet, despite the
apparent confusion, townsmen in Uganda cope with these circumstances and establish social order. This study describes the
strategy by which they do so.

Stratification and Friendship

This strategy will be examined as it operates in the friendships of Africans in Mbale, Uganda. Mbale is a multi-ethnic
administrative and commercial regional center with a population of approximately 20,000. Its two functional bases underlie
the socio-economic division of its African population into two
major categories: one composed of relatively well educated and
highly paid senior civil servants and other high-ranking
bureaucrats; the other composed primarily of unskilled laborers who are uneducated and poor. In this study, these two
categories will be called "elite" and "non-elite," respectively,
following the terms used in African urban studies, or, alterna-
tively, "upper class" and "lower class," following the usage of
Africans in Mbale.[1]

This study focuses on the elite Africans, although some
consideration is given to the other Africans in the town. This
emphasis derives in part from an effort to help fill a gap in
studies of African urban life. Most urban studies in Africa have
described African townsmen who fall into the lower-class
category, although they refer, if only briefly, and indirectly, to
those in another, elite, class. For example, the Sofers in their
study of Jinja, Uganda, describe non-elite Africans for the most
part, but they identify another class of Africans—the "professionals"—who are relatively well educated and more highly
paid than the "porters" (i.e., unskilled laborers), and who
confine their friendships to their own group (Sofer and Sofer
1955: 39, 46, 69). Again, Southall, writing of Africans in Kisenyi, a suburb of Kampala, Uganda's capital, describes the social
life of lower-class Africans but indicates the existence of upper-class Africans who look down on Kisenyi as a "slum"
(Southall and Gutkind 1956:19).

The focus on friendship in this study derives not only
from the social science literature, but also from the exigencies

---

[1]My use of the terms "elite" and "non-elite" follows that of P.C.
Lloyd (1966:4). See his discussion of the advantages and limitations
of their use (Ibid., 49–62).

of social life in Mbale. In the former, the distinction between
persons unknown and known, between uncertainty and certainty, is often typified as the difference between stranger and
friend (*see* Wood 1934). Denzin, for example, contrasts the
relationship between strangers, the fleeting and potentially
dangerous encounter between the unacquainted, with friendship, which one enters with feelings of confidence and safety
(Denzin 1970:70). Two other reasons for studying friendship
in particular follow from the nature of social life among Africans in Mbale. First, interaction with friends dominates their
leisure activities. Most Africans in the town are itinerants; they
work and live in Mbale before moving on, either to jobs in
other urban centers or to their homes elsewhere in Uganda; few
have any ties of a permanent nature within the town itself.[2]
Their interaction with one another, outside the work situation
and its constraints, is primarily as friends, rather than as kinsmen or neighbors. Secondly, their ideas about friendship underlie the fact that they interact in leisure time at all. Since the
Africans in Mbale do not have any particular commitments in
the town, it is conceivable that they could participate only in
necessary occupational and economic relationships, without
becoming otherwise involved with one another. However, despite these obstacles, their culture of friendship, including the
significance which they attach to sociability, brings them
together.

Description and Analysis

One of the major difficulties in studying urban social order
comes in the attempt to analyze and describe interactional
regularities within a complex and unstable social field. Previ-
ous studies of African townsmen have tended to deal with this

---

[2]My use of the term "itinerants" follows in part that of Hughes
(1958); Whyte (1956) uses the word "transients" and Watson (1964)
suggests the term "spiralists" to describe individuals similar to those
who in this study are referred to as "upper-class" itinerants. The term
"migrant" is more usually applied to "lower-class" itinerants.

problem by focusing on the structure and function of corporate groups, primarily voluntary associations. The emphasis on such groups often reflects two influences: first, an inclination on the part of social anthropologists, who were among the first to carry out social research in urban Africa, to study those structural units with which they were by training and experience most familiar, and secondly, an effort simply to isolate for study organizational entities which were relatively discrete and enduring, in contrast to the less formal and more transient (and difficult to record) social relationships in urban life.

An emphasis on corporate groups, however, is impractical in urban situations like that of Mbale. In Mbale, African participation in voluntary associations and other corporate groups is minimal. Therefore it is necessary to use other methods to study social organization. Network analysis, in particular, has proved to be a useful analytical and descriptive tool for this problem. It provides a technique and a context for the study of social relationships among individuals who are incorporated into social life without membership in corporate groups.

Describing the structure of social relations and the networks which they constitute is, however, only part of the problem. It is still necessary to interpret them and to determine the conditions under which they persist. This requires further analysis. A common research strategy in social anthropology is to isolate and describe interactional patterns among a specific population and to explain these patterns in terms of the population's cultural system (*e.g.,* their values, norms and beliefs) and their non-normative environment. Interactional data— who interacts with whom in what ways and in which contexts —may be gathered directly through observation (with or without participation) on the part of the researcher and indirectly through the use of interview schedules and questionnaires; and they are amenable to quantitative analysis. The interpretation of these interactional data proceeds by means of cultural analysis, which involves an examination of the premises which constitute the underlying logical structure of the cultural system. The premises are inferred primarily from what informants say, and particularly from their explanations and analyses of their own social life. Cultural analysis does not depend on quantitative techniques, but rather it requires study of the meaning of key concepts in the cultural system. Although non-normative factors, in this particular case primarily occupational opportunities and economic resources, are studied to determine their effect on the alternative course of action open to informants, cultural analysis focuses on normative factors which constrain and facilitate interaction, that is, on the principles which lie behind decision-making in social action.

One example of the interplay between cultural and interactional analyses involves the social division between elite and non-elite Africans in Mbale. That division is fully intelligible only in terms of the elite's ideas about stratification and friendship. Although there is a clear interactional separation between elite and non-elite Africans (elite friendships being contained exclusively within the elite), it is difficult to draw the boundary between the two groups simply in terms of socio-economic attributes. For, although some elite Africans earn an income not much greater than that of some non-elite Africans, they are still included among the elite both cognitively and interactionally. In this case, they are educated, up-and-coming young men who will be able to participate, over time, in the reciprocities expected in elite friendship behavior. For non-elite Africans, including those older men whose maximum earnings are comparable to the young elite Africans' starting salaries, the prospects of an increasing future income are extremely slight, and their potential for meeting the costs involved in elite friendship is practically non-existent. To understand the position of these young elite men requires knowledge of the elite's values, norms, and beliefs, that is, their culture of social stratification and friendship.

Field Site and Informants

The field data on which this study is based were collected in Mbale, Uganda between the beginning of October, 1965 and the end of August, 1966. The description of social life there

applies to that period, unless otherwise noted. Several anthropological studies (Sofer and Sofer 1955, Southall and Gutkind 1956, and Parkin 1969) have been conducted in Uganda's
urban centers, providing a base for the research described in
this book. None of these focus on elite Africans in a regional,
rather than a national, capital. In this respect, the study of
Africans in Mbale offers data for comparative analysis. Mbale's status as a regional headquarters and a secondary population center, however, also present certain problems for a
comparison of African urban life in Uganda. For example, the
relatively limited number and undifferentiated nature of occupational opportunities for lower-class Africans in Mbale tends
to underscore the division between them and those in the
upper class. That is, there are fewer middle-range jobs in either
public service or private industry for Africans in Mbale than
there are in Kampala. Further, there has not yet emerged in the
former as there has in the latter, a distinct "middle class,"
either numerically or interactionally, which might fit *between*,
and perhaps mediate between, the elite and the non-elite. Most
of the Africans in Kampala, studied by Parkin (1969) and described by him as "middle class" (*Ibid.*,ix,89), would, in Mbale,
fall, at least socio-economically, into the non-elite category,
although in other respects they seem to lie between Mbale's
elite and non-elite. Parkin, however, notes that there are
"higher status" individuals (those he labels "upper middle
class") who do not participate in the social lives of "middle-
class Africans" (*Ibid.*,103, 153). It seems likely that these up-
per-middle-class men would be part of the upper class in
Mbale. At the other end of the scale, since there are few elite
Africans in Mbale who are self-employed or who are influential politicians, compared to the large number who are senior
civil servants and public officials, the differentiation possible
within the upper class tends to be played down. However, as
will be seen, there seems little doubt that most elite Africans
in Mbale are part of a nation-wide network of upper-class
Africans.

   At the time of the research, Mbale's African elite consisted
of a core of some 125 men. In the course of field work, almost

all of these men were contacted. These contacts ranged from short interviews with most of them, through more detailed interviews with about half of them, to ties of friendship, which involved intensive and continuous participation, with about thirty men. These friendships, which were with individuals in different sets of friends, were maintained throughout the research.

A number of sources were used in the identification and selection of elite informants. One of the major sources of information was the Ugandan government's *Enumeration of Employees* (1965), which indicated that in 1964 there were 107 Africans, 82 in public service and 25 in private industry, working in Mbale who earned $1680 or more per year. This figure seemed a likely place to begin looking for "elite" Africans, since it represented the top 2 percent wage-earners in the town. Although the enumeration was from the year before field work, it also seemed likely that the figure would be about the same in 1965-66, since the number of occupational positions at that income level would probably remain fairly constant. (In fact, the 1965 enumeration, published in November, 1966, indicated that the number of men had increased by only 4, all public service employees.) A second source was the Mbale Municipal Council's graduated tax (poll tax) register, listing those males 18 and older residing within Mbale and assessed for taxes. This list, unlike the central government's *Enumeration*, contains the *names* of individuals and the amount of tax they are assessed, which is based on their annual income. The assessment rate, however, indicates only the range of income, since only the first $1680 is assessed for this tax. That is, a man's income up to $1680 could be inferred from the assessment; if he earned more, he was still taxed at the $1680 level. The tax register includes those employed both in public service and in private industry. A third source of names was the list of occupants of government housing, both central and local, since those eligible for this housing usually have an annual income of at least $1680. The tax register and the housing list yielded the names of 92 men; I was unable to discover why the other 15 men were not included on either of them. Questioning these 92 men about their friends, and checking their statements by observation of friendship interactional patterns, produced the names of another 33 men. Their incomes were less than $1680, but they were included, both cognitively and interactionally, within the elite. I conducted interviews with 84 percent (105) of this total of 125 men. The other 20 men were not interviewed, either because they were unavailable (for example, several men who were scheduled to be interviewed were transferred away from Mbale during the course of field work and before they could be seen) or because of oversights in the field work process.

To complement the study of Mbale's African elite, data were collected about non-elite Africans in the town. The non-elite are divided between those who live on the housing estates (municipally-controlled housing developments) and those who live elsewhere in the town, including its less developed rural areas. From those on the housing estates, fifty male household heads were selected and interviewed with the same interview schedules that were used with approximately the same number of elite Africans. The housing estate sample is not a random one; it is, however, typical of the total housing estate population with respect to education, occupation, and income. It was selected to provide a comparison with the elite: non-elite Africans are similar ethnically to elite Africans, but dissimilar socio-economically.

Non-elite Africans not living on the housing estates are represented in this study by data also derived from a small sample. Ten male household heads were selected from each of five "village" areas within the town and were interviewed with the same schedule that was used with the elite Africans and with those non-elite Africans living on the housing estates. Again, those selected were not randomly chosen: each set of 10 were neighbors, and the specific data available about these people are derived primarily from these fifty "villagers." There is, however, a similarity between this sample and the rest of the population in the town's rural area in terms of occupation and income.

These approximately 200 people are the informants from

whom specific data were obtained for this study. Fullest data were collected from and about the African elite, which is the focus of the study; and more limited data were collected, for comparative purposes, from and about Africans who are in the non-elite category.

Abstract and Outline

Africans in Mbale are itinerant townsmen. The upper-class Africans, for their working lives, are urban-based and move, because of job transfers, from one town to another. Non-elite Africans, for economic reasons, must circulate between town and countryside, to supplement their meager incomes with subsistence farming and cash-cropping. The geographical mobility of both classes of townsmen produces a state of uncertainty which undermines their social relationships. To cope with this uncertainty, they confine their relationships to those with whom they expect continuity of association, which requires their perception implicitly or explicitly of the conditions which will result in their recurrent interaction. Although there are structural differences, their cultural foundations are formally similar. Common to both classes is a future orientation which supports interaction within their respective networks. Elite Africans expect to see one another over time in the various urban centers of Uganda. Non-elite Africans of different tribal backgrounds expect to see fellow tribesmen in their tribal homelands. In both cases, an expectation of future interaction lends credibility to present association, despite its recognized short-term duration. Their belief about interaction, over time, including the establishment, dissolution, and renewal of social relationships, serve to maintain social order within the urban context.

Chapter Two contains a description of Mbale Municipality and its population. The socio-economic and ethnic heterogencity and geographical mobility which characterize Mbale's residents suggest its appropriateness as a test case for the study of urbanism. It also provides a profile of the African population, including the socio-economic and tribal attributes of elite and non-elite Africans.

Chapter Three examines social stratification among Mbale's African population. Their ideas about social class structure conceptualize their socio-economic differences and provide a context for their friendship culture and interaction. This chapter also describes the social boundaries of the elite in the context of leisure-time interaction, illustrating that ideas have behavioral consequences. It also explores the division between elite Africans and non-African elites.

Chapter Four analyzes the culture of friendship within the two classes. It focuses on the rights and duties of friendship, on the assumption that reciprocity is necessary in friendship interaction, on the idea that friendship should be between social equals, and on the cultural meanings of social equality. The beliefs, values, and norms about friendship make friendship choices intelligible.

Chapter Five describes friendship choices. Among elite Africans, common status and common occupation are primary factors, while tribal identity is not. Among non-elite Africans, common tribe is of primary significance. The structure of friendship confirms the significance of cultural analysis: economic constraints may explain the exclusion of non-elite Africans from the costly friendship behavior of elite Africans, but they do not explain the decision of elite Africans, with their greater wealth, to avoid the non-elite in their friendships.

Chapter Six presents a model of the conditions which promote and impede social solidarity. One significant sociological condition for solidarity appears to be a sense of certainty about the future of a relationship. Certainty, in turn, is based on estimates of the probability, both statistical and social, of future association. The importance among the elite of a common career, and among the non-elite of a tribal fellowship, reflects conditions conducive to future association. The differential emphasis on colleagueship and tribalism in the friendship choices of the two classes can be seen as strategies for managing uncertainty.

Chapter Seven presents a cross-cultural comparison of the management of uncertainty in urban situations. Two cases, one from West Africa and one from America, illustrate similarities in the strategy used by Africans in Uganda for adapting to the circumstances of urban life.

The Conclusion contains a summary of the argument and raises questions which follow from it that are relevant to problems of wider interest in urban anthropology.

CHAPTER TWO

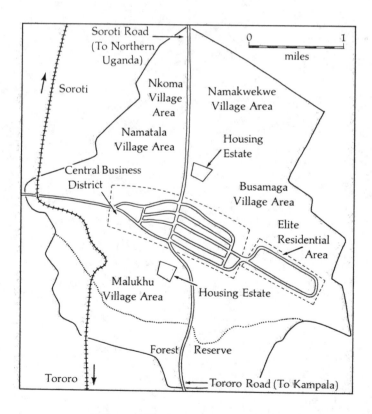

Map 2. Sketch-map of the Mbale Municipality

Mbale Municipality

Mbale is located in eastern Uganda, 170 miles northeast of Kampala, the nation's capital and largest city. By comparison to Kampala, it is a relatively small regional center and therefore might seem not large enough to find the problems usually associated with urbanism as a way of life. Yet, there are a number of factors other than size which, by themselves and in combination, produce among its population a sense of anonymity and uncertainty and a potential for social disorder.

Size and Population Growth

Mbale follows Kampala and Jinja in population size, but the figures available do not accurately reflect the number of Africans in the town. In 1965, according to a census conducted by the local government, Mbale had an estimated population of 20,000, of whom 15,000 were Africans and the rest were mostly "Asians," those of Indian or Pakistani descent.[1] The figure of 15,000 Africans includes 11,000 resident within the

---

[1] The "Asians" of Mbale, although a significant minority in the town's population, are not the concern of this study. Their relationships with Africans are formal and largely limited to business transactions. In many respects the Asians constitute, at least to the town's Africans, a single group, although they are in fact divided into several distinct "communities" (see Morris 1968).

15

town proper and at least another 4,000 who live just outside
the town's boundaries, but who come into Mbale daily for
work. It does not include those from the surrounding hinterland who come into Mbale, also daily, to use its commercial,
medical, and recreational facilities and services.

The size of Mbale's African population is probably under-
estimated, for several reasons. The most important of these is
that the figure of 11,000 is an estimate of the municipality's tax
collectors, and does not include an apparently considerable
number of men who avoid being "discovered" and assessed by
them. Secondly, there are an undetermined number of transients, mostly tribesmen from the surrounding hinterland, who
stay within the town for shorter or longer periods of time but
who are not counted by the local authorities as residents because they do not pay taxes to the municipality. Thirdly, there
are a number of individuals, mostly Gisu tribesmen, from one
of the adjacent administrative districts who live in one of Mbale's outlying undeveloped areas and claim that it does not
belong to the town but to their tribal district. According to one
municipal officer, the tribesmen often defend their claim with
force. The town's police and tax collectors are reluctant to go
there, so it is unlikely that these people are included within the
census. Although some of these reasons may be particular to
Mbale, a downward bias, as Hance notes (1970:5–15), seems to
be a general feature of African census data.

Mbale is a rapidly growing town. In 1948, Mbale had an
African population of about 3,700; by 1959, there were about
8,500 Africans. This represents an increase of approximately
125 percent, or close to an annual cumulative increase of 8
percent. Even if the low estimate of 11,000 is used, by 1965 the
rate of growth had continued at nearly 6 percent per year.
Thus, in less than 20 years, Mbale's African population has
almost tripled.

The size and the growth rate of the town's population,
however, seem to be the least important factors in producing
those characteristics commonly associated with urbanism as a
way of life. Rather, socio-economic and ethnic heterogeneity
and geographical mobility divide the town's population into a
mosaic of separate social worlds, each marked by rapid popula-

tion turnover, each seeming, as Epstein suggests (1964:83), a "phantasmagoria," a changing scene of diverse individuals constantly appearing and disappearing.

Economy and Social Composition

Mbale is an administrative and commercial center. It is the headquarters of the central government in eastern Uganda, housing regional offices for departments of administration, medicine and public health, agriculture, education, post and communications, and police. It also contains a large hospital, training schools for health inspectors and medical assistants, and a senior secondary school, all run by the central government. Furthermore, it is the seat of administration for both Bugisu and Bukedi Districts, which surround the town. Mbale also has its own administration.

In addition to its status as an administrative center for regional, district, and local levels, Mbale is a commercial and distributional center for eastern and much of northern Uganda (see O'Connor 1965:45–46). Three cooperative unions have their main offices in the town, including one which handles coffee production for Bugisu District and two others which market cotton production for both Bugisu and Bukedi Districts. The coffee co-operative also has a coffee processing plant in Mbale. Several international oil companies (Esso, Caltex, Shell, Agip) have their depots and administrative offices in the town; and a number of hides and skins companies have their offices, tanneries, and warehouses there as well. Mbale also has some light industry, primarily the processing of cotton oil and cotton seed by-products and maize meal. A municipally-operated market and a large number of shops serve the town's population as well as that of the surrounding districts. A part of Mbale's economy is also based on an entertainment industry, which includes almost fifty bars and several movie theatres.

The two functional bases, administration and commerce, provide a range of occupational opportunities for Mbale's Africans and underlie their division into an elite and a non-elite. Most elite Africans in Mbale are senior civil servants. They are regional, district, and local administrators, doctors, educational supervisors and inspectors, agricultural advisors, and police officials. Some others are managers in the co-operative unions, in public corporations such as the Uganda Electricity Board, and in the international business firms which have offices in the town. There are no politicians among the elite Africans in Mbale, a fact which is related, as will be seen, to the town's particular administrative organization. In contrast to the elite, most Africans in Mbale are workers with only limited skills. Only 10 percent of male adult African employees in Mbale are "skilled" workers, according to the central government's 1964 *Enumeration of Employees,* and most of the nonelite Africans are unskilled laborers.

This division between an elite composed of senior civil servants and a non-elite composed of unskilled laborers is so pronounced in Mbale because there are few elite Africans in private enterprise. In Mbale, as elsewhere in Uganda, Asians control commerce (see Davis 1962, Fallers 1964, Morris 1968). For example, Asians own 85 percent of Mbale's rateable property (that which is under long-term lease and subject to property tax) which includes most of its shops, garages, and bars.

In addition to the Asian control of commerce, there are two other important reasons why the majority of elite Africans are civil servants. This pattern stems partly from the fact that Uganda was primarily a political, rather than an economic, colony (Fallers 1964:125). Britain extended its control over the Ugandan protectorate through politics and administration, rather than through industry and commerce. And since the relatively complex administrative structure was imposed on a near subsistence economy, the government controlled not only the public services but also the development and marketing of cash-crops. The senior civil service did and does still provide a standard of power and prestige for educated Africans. The pattern also derives from the fact that under British rule the structure and content of higher education in Uganda was designed specifically to train Africans for public service. As Goldthorpe indicates, the British wanted highly educated Africans as teachers, as medical personnel, as staff for the agricultural services, and, from the years directly preceding independence, as high-level administrators (Goldthorpe 1965:63).

The division between elite and non-elite Africans in occupations is reflected in the differences between them in other socio-economic characteristics. Elite Africans are relatively well-educated: 30 percent have been to college, most (76 percent) have completed secondary school, and practically all (98 percent) have completed junior secondary school. Of those who are university trained, about 50 percent went to Makerere University College in Uganda and all but four of the others went to schools in the United Kingdom. They are also relatively wealthy; the elite's average annual cash income is about $2700 and 75 percent earn more than $1960.[2] In these respects, the elite Africans in Mbale appear to be typical of Uganda's African elite. Goldthorpe, for example, writes that more than 50 percent of Uganda's highly educated Africans work for the central government and that the great majority of them earn more than $1960 per year (*Ibid.*, 61, 67). In contrast to the elite, non-elite Africans are relatively uneducated. None have completed secondary school and 60 percent have not completed primary school. They are relatively poor; the average cash income per year of the non-elite Africans sampled is about $400, and according to the 1964 *Enumeration of Employees*, 92 percent of all adult male Africans working in Mbale earn less than $672 per year.[3]

The sharp contrast between elite and non-elite Africans is consistent with the occupational structure of Africans in Mbale. The correlation between education, occupation, and income is related to the absence of opportunity for Africans in

---

[2] I have translated from Ugandan to United States currency unless otherwise noted.

[3] Although the non-elite Africans in Mbale are poor in comparison with its elite population, they are relatively wealthy when compared to the tribesmen living in the rural districts which surround the town. Davis notes that in 1959 the cash income per head throughout the eastern region (then province) was $28 (Davis 1962:442), and the agricultural officer for Bugisu District estimated that in 1965 the average income to coffee growers from Bugisu's coffee crop was $70 (personal communication).

business and trade, where formal education is not necessary for financial success. It is also related to the nature of the bureaucracies for which elite Africans work. In the civil service, as well as in the private large-scale corporations, high educational qualification is generally prerequisite to high-ranking position, which in turn is related to high income level. Moreover, the great disparity in incomes between the two classes is, like the concentration of elite Africans in the civil service, a legacy of colonial rule. The salaries of senior civil servants are based on what they had been, prior to independence, for expatriate officers whose pay was adjusted to the standards of their home country (see Lloyd 1966:10–11).

Both the elite and the non-elite are tribally heterogeneous. The elite includes Acholi, Ankole, Ganda, Gisu, Gwere, Kiga, Padhola, Soga, and Teso. Although the Ganda are the largest single category, comprising about 30 percent of the elite Africans in the town, each of the other tribal categories comprises between 5 percent and 15 percent of the elite population. The lower-class Africans also are divided into a number of different tribal groupings, but the tribesmen from the surrounding districts predominate. Mbale is located near three tribal districts (Bugisu, Bukedi and Teso), and it draws most of its non-elite Africans from these hinterland areas. Gisu and people from Bukedi Districts, primarily Gwere, constitute about 50 percent of the town's lower-class population, with Gisu forming just over half that number. Soga comprise another 15 percent, while Teso, Ganda, and Acholi each contribute about 10 percent of the population. The remaining non-elite Africans in the town are from Kenya.

One consequence of the tribal complexity of Mbale's African population is the diversity of languages spoken in the town. In Uganda, the African languages are divided into three major groups, which are mutually unintelligible. When a number of languages from each of these groups are spoken simultaneously, as is often the case in lower-class bars, confusion reigns. In contrast to the non-elite Africans who do not share a common language, all the elite Africans speak English. In Uganda, English is the medium of instruction in secondary schools and of communication in the central government, as

well as in para-government organizations and large-scale private firms. In Mbale, English is also the official language of
municipal government. Although English is not the established
language in the administrations of the Districts which border
on Mbale, men in senior positions there use English in their
contacts with the municipal and central government officers.
Elite Africans also speak English in their leisure hours.

Housing and Town Layout

In addition to its socio-economic and ethnic differences,
Mbale's African population is also divided residentially. The
different areas of housing provide a concrete expression of the
separate worlds in which Africans live. Mbale has an area of
approximately nine square miles, of which about one-third is
"developed" and the rest, including a little less than two square
miles of forest preserve, is not. The developed area is characterized by the Town Engineer as "built-up, with permanent
buildings, water, sewerage, tarmac roads, electricity, and street
lighting." It contains the municipal market, hospital, post
office, police station, secondary school, business offices, food,
drug, and clothing stores, banks, bars, gas stations, and the
various offices of regional, district, and local administration. It
also contains the homes of many Asian families, some of
whom live in apartments over their stores and shops. Physically, it is the most recognizably "urban" area in the town (see
Plates 1 and 2).

It is also the most urban in its admixture of people. It is
the scene of bustling crowds, made up not only of civil servants
and merchants, but also of shoppers, beggers, and men out of
work (see Plates 3–6). The occupational diversity of the people
is matched by the variety in their clothing. Upper-class men,
African and non-African both, dress in suit and tie or slacks
and shirts. Lower-class men also dress in slacks and shirts, but
these are usually torn and shabby. They also wear khaki shirts
and shorts, and sometimes an older man dons a *kanzu,* a floor-
length shirt-like gown. Most Asian women wear saris, some
wear Western dresses. African women wear *basutis,* billowy

Plate 1. Clock Tower and Central Plaza

Plate 2. A Main Street

Plate 3. Asian Shop and African Townsmen

Plate 4. Street-corner Conversation

Plate 5. Milton Obote Avenue

Plate 6. Midday Shoppers

maternity-like dresses, a legacy of Victorian-minded mission-aries, intended to conceal the female form. The wives of elite Africans wear basutis made of fine materials, lower-class women wear ones made of ordinary cotton. Women of both classes wear Western dresses, although those of the wives of elite men are made of more costly material and are less worn-out than those of lower-class women. It is not unusual for lower-class Africans, men and women, to go shoeless.

Also within the developed area, but removed from the central business district, are the homes of upper-class Africans and others of similar status. They live in what the town brochure describes as the "high-class residential area." Most elite Africans live in homes owned by either the central or local governments or by the national and international firms; their housing is tied to their jobs. The central government's requirements for access to its housing is that a person hold a position which has a salary minimum of $1960 per year, although this standard is occasionally modified by consideration of marital status, number of dependents, and years of service. The municipal government's policy concerning eligibility for its housing is generally the same as that of the central government, as is that of the district governments, oil companies, and co-operative unions. A few banks and other companies also have a small number of houses which they occasionally lease to private persons, but the rents are so high as to virtually exclude all but those of elite status.

The upper-class residential area resembles a middle-class suburban neighborhood in the United States. Its paved roads are broad and tree-shaded; the houses are constructed of stucco and brick, with tile roofing, and they are set on large plots of land, surrounded by well kept lawns and gardens (see Plate 7). The houses range in size from three to five bedrooms. All of them have spacious living rooms and modern bathrooms and kitchens, the latter equipped with electric appliances (see Plate 8). Government housing is uniformly furnished: beds, dining-room table and chairs, couch, and armchairs. Individual families are expected to supply their own "soft furnishings": sheets, blankets, towels, curtains, and other linen goods. This uniformity, however, does not preclude variations in furnishings.

Plate 7. Elite Neighborhood

Plate 8. Elite House

27

For example, one family had added another couch and two more armchairs, a phonograph, a large radio, and a bookcase filled with "mysteries," a copy of Dr. Spock's child-care manual, and a number of books related to the man's profession. There was also a collection of long-playing records, including a number of Jim Reeves' albums, very popular in Uganda, and one copy of the Mormon Tabernacle Choir in concert with the Philadelphia Orchestra, conducted by Eugene Ormandy.

Most of the elite Africans who reside in these houses live in nuclear families. Almost 80 percent of the elite Africans are married, and approximately the same proportion of the married elite men live with their wives and young children. Most of their older children past primary-school age leave home to attend secondary school, for the most part boarding schools in Uganda. Their married children do not live with them. Another 10 percent of the married men have nieces or nephews staying with them temporarily; these are students who are enrolled at Mbale's senior secondary school. If an elite family is transferred, the students move back into school-provided accommodations. The other elite families, also about 10 percent, also have a relative living with them, usually a young girl who works around the house as either a domestic or a nursemaid.

Non-elite Africans are separated from elite Africans and live on housing estates and in the town's undeveloped area. The housing estates, municipally controlled housing developments, are situated on the edges of the town's developed area, divided from the homes of the elite Africans by the center of town. There are 262 houses on two estates. Most of them are built of concrete blocks, and most have tile roofing, although some have tin sheeting (see Plate 9). They are set on small plots, separated by a few yards of dirt or grass. The houses vary in size from one to three rooms; "cooking areas" are outside and behind the houses, as are outhouses. The estates are not fully supplied with the urban amenities: they have no street lighting, only some of the houses are supplied with water or electricity, and only a few of the houses have indoor plumbing. Most (85 percent) lower-class Africans live in the undeveloped areas of Mbale. Housing there resembles that in rural villages (see Plate 10). Indeed, there are five named "village" areas which are officially recognized by the Mbale Municipal Coun-

Plate 9. Non-elite Compound

Plate 10. Non-elite Village in Town

cil (in its Register of Voters). The rural areas do not have paved roads, electricity, piped water other than a few widely scattered communal taps, or a water-borne sewage system. The houses are not permanent, being constructed usually of mud and wattle with either tinsheet or thatch roofing. The house-type varies with the tribal background of the occupant of the house.

Many Africans living in these villages-within-the-town are cultivators. They lease plots of land from the municipality, under a system of annually renewable "Temporary Occupation Licenses" (TOL). The TOL's are of two kinds: "Urban User" and "Agriculture and Residence Only." An 'Urban User' permit allows an individual to have on his plot either a shop, a native beer bar, or tenants. An "Agriculture and Residence Only" permit allows a man to build his own home and to have a small garden for subsistence agriculture and a limited amount of cash-cropping. The division by type of TOL indicates the general occupational structure of the Africans living in this area. Of 605 names in the Mbale Municipal Council's 1965–66 TOL Register, about 16 percent (109) are listed as having "Urban User" permits, and the remaining 84 percent (496) have "Agriculture and Residence" permits.

A majority of the non-elite Africans residing in Mbale do not live in nuclear families. Of the non-elite men 86 percent are married; of those, more than half (53 percent) live with people in addition to their wives and children. Almost 40 percent of the "extra-familial" residents are brothers or sisters of either the head of the household or his wife; another 14 percent are (first) cousins of either the husband or the wife; another 6 percent are their nieces and nephews; and another 25 percent comprise more distant relatives. Non-relatives, usually fellow tribesmen, make up 15 percent of the extra-familial residents.

Social and Administrative History

The socio-economic and ethnic heterogeneity which characterizes Mbale is not only a reflection of its current geographical situation and functional bases but also a product of its development for the past sixty years. Mbale's history begins in

1902, the year in which a Ganda "chief," Semei Kakungulu, founded a settlement at what is now the modern town.[4] The British administration used Ganda soldiers and adventurers, like Kakungulu, to "pacify" native populations beyond the immediate control of the protectorate government which was located in Kampala. Kakungulu, in the employ of the British, conquered a large part of the eastern half of Uganda in the years before the turn of the century. As part of the compensation for his services, officials of the British Protectorate granted Kakungulu, in 1902, 20 square miles of freehold land in the area of present-day Mbale, and he "retired" there with his followers, mostly Ganda, but also some Soga and Gwere, to establish a settlement. The site chosen by Kakungulu for reasons of defense and diet was before his arrival apparently an uninhabited and unoccupied region of waste land. Even then, however, tribesmen from the surrounding areas, particularly Gisu, Gwere and Teso, fought for control of the land. From its earliest beginnings, Mbale has been tribally heterogeneous.

The founding of Mbale by Kakungulu and his followers helps to account for the many Ganda living in the town: they are either the survivors or the descendants of Kakungulu's following. Furthermore, the followers of Kakungulu and their descendants who live in Mbale today reside in the rural areas of the town—indeed, they have seen the town's boundaries grow up around them—and are administered by Mbale's Municipal Agent (formerly known as the Township Chief), who is one of Kakungulu's sons.

The founding of Mbale also throws light on its emergence as a commercial and administrative center. When Kakungulu and his followers settled at Mbale they quickly undertook intensive cultivation of plantains to meet their daily needs. In addition, they began to trade with the local tribes for other food, wood and building essentials. Another item traded in Kakungulu's Mbale was ivory, which had an even more significant influence on the town's development. In the years

---

[4]My account of Mbale's history draws heavily on Twaddle's "The Founding of Mbale" (1966) and on Government documents (O'Connor 1962).

immediately following Kakungulu's arrival in the area, the ivory trade brought to Mbale non-African traders, who came to acquire that valuable commodity then being collected in the Karamoja plains to the north of Mbale. Mbale became the main staging center for caravans to the north. As a result of both the size of Kakungulu's following and the aggregation of local tribesmen who traded ivory with the non-Africans, the population of Mbale was estimated to be between 2,000 and 3,000 in 1904. This represented a potential retail market which attracted even more traders. It is estimated that by the beginning of 1904, Mbale had the largest trading bazaar in Uganda outside the protectorate capital. Furthermore, Mbale had become such a thriving center that it was made the site of an administrative station by the Protectorate government, also in 1904. Thus, from its beginnings, Mbale has exhibited some of the characteristics which mark its current scene: an administrative and commercial center, occupationally differentiated, ethnically heterogeneous, with its trade controlled by non-Africans.

Mbale's history since 1904 throws still more light on its current administrative and social structures. The town's present status as an independent administrative unit is rooted in a complex history, but much of it can be summarized as a process of adjustment between the conflicting claims for the land of Mbale by the Gwere and Gisu, whose tribal territories surround the town. In 1906 the Protectorate's administration in Mbale was established as a Township encompassing the area within a two-mile radius from the Collector's Office, near the site of the present building of Mbale's Municipal Council. In 1923 Bugisu and Bugwere Districts were formed; Bugwere District headquarters was established in Mbale and that of Bugisu outside the town. This action was resented by the Gisu, who felt they were being cheated of their traditional land. In 1937 for reasons of economy the British consolidated Bugisu and Bugwere Districts as Central District with headquarters in Mbale. In 1941, Bugisu and Bukedi Districts, the latter including Bugwere, were carved out of the older administrative unit. Mbale township was given a "new status," to be treated as "federal territory" under the jurisdiction of neither Native Administration (O'Connor 1962:6–7). Thus, the central government found that declaring Mbale a neutral territory was a way of circumventing the conflicting claims of Gwere and Gisu tribesmen.

The developments since 1941 further shaped Mbale's present situation. In 1949 Bugisu and Bukedi Districts became African Local Governments and their administrative offices were built in Mbale. In 1954, Mbale became a Township District; also at that time a Mbale Township District Council and an Urban District Council were created. In effect, the Township District Council was concerned with African interests and the Urban District Council with non-African interests. The division in administrative units reflected the separation between Asians and Europeans in the developed part of the town and the Africans in its rural parts. In 1958 the Urban District Council became a Town Council, and in 1960 the Mbale Township District Council and the Mbale Town Council were merged when African members of the District Council were appointed to the Town Council. In 1962, on the country's independence, Mbale was designated a Municipality. Thus, Mbale has evolved as a separate administrative unit, although its boundaries and claims on its land have been continually disputed by the neighboring Gwere and Gisu.

Today Mbale is an independent municipality. It is also a "township territory," which means that its land is controlled by the central government rather than by a tribal authority or district administration. When Uganda gained its independence, all land except certain freehold areas was put under the authority of the Land Boards of the districts into which the country was divided. The Land Boards were obligated to lease the land on which towns were situated to their ruling authorities, the municipal and town councils. In 1962, however, both Bugisu and Bukedi Districts claimed the land of Mbale for their respective administrations. Instead of awarding the disputed land to either District, the central government proclaimed Mbale to be a federal territory, as it had in 1941. The land was vested in the President of Uganda, to be administered by the central government's Commissioner of Lands and Surveys acting as agent for the President.

Today, the central government controls the acquisition

and use of land in Mbale. To acquire land in Mbale, application is made to the Commissioner of Lands and Surveys whose office is located in Kampala, through his representative, a senior civil servant, posted in Mbale. The Department of Lands and Surveys through its local representative and his staff evaluates the plot. Considering the type of building to be erected on the site, the Department fixes land premiums, rents, and other taxes and then submits this report to the town council. The council has the option of approving or disapproving, but the Department's report is the final word on valuation and rent.

Not only does the central government control land in Mbale, but it also controls the town's general administration and politics. Most of the Mbale Municipal Council's financing comes from the central government; and the central government controls the town's administration through the Mbale Municipal Council's annual budget, its estimates of income and expenditure, which is subject to approval by the Ministry of Regional Administration. Approval from the central government must also be obtained for the borrowing of money, for the content of by-laws, and for the exercise of many of the Council's powers. The Ministry of Regional Administration also controls the town's political life, since it appoints or approves the appointment of the town's Mayor, its Deputy Mayor, its Councillors, and its administrative officers. Thus, the major decisions about Mbale's operation are made in Kampala; the local administration's job is to implement the directives of the central government. Service as a Councillor does not confer elite status. Those Councillors who are of elite status are so on other grounds; the Mayor, for example, is also a magistrate, appointed by the central government.

Geographical Mobility

Although socio-economic and ethnic differences as expressed in residential distribution divide Africans in Mbale, their geographical mobility is most important in producing anonymity and uncertainty among them. It is conceivable that the in-migration of Mbale's African population could have resulted in an aggregation of a number of separate "communities," each characterized by socio-economic and tribal homogeneity and residential stability. In short, Mbale could have become a composite of urban villages, with residential stability and social solidarity marking life within, if not between, them. In fact, this is the pattern of social life among the cultivators, those survivors and descendants of Kakungulu's followers, who live in the rural areas of the town. They are, virtually, urban villagers. But the rest of Mbale's Africans are geographically mobile; and their movement separates them from kin, neighbors, and friends, who are dispersed between different urban centers and rural hinterlands throughout Uganda. It also brings them into contact with strangers, making the town a place full of people unknown and potentially dangerous to one another.

Both the elite and the non-elite Africans are itinerant townsmen. The elite Africans work in large-scale organizations which transfer their senior employees regularly and frequently, moving them between towns which are the centers of government administration and commercial management. For example, it is the central government's policy that any senior civil servant can be transferred at any time to any place, except that senior officers are usually not posted to their "home" areas. Consequently, most (73 percent) of the elite Africans in Mbale had worked and lived in the town for less than three years.

Their turnover, moreover, is often quite sudden: within a six-month period of field work, almost 40 percent of the senior civil servants have been transferred from Mbale, disrupting not only their work lives but also their social relationships. One informant, for example, was sent by the government from Mbale to England for a six-month's course of study. When he returned to the town, all of his friends had been transferred to other urban centers. Moreover, elite Africans are often given no more than two weeks notice before they are expected to be at their new post, and they do not know beforehand where the next post will be or how long their stay in any particular place will last. With the frequency of their moves, most elite Africans had worked and lived in more than three different towns in Uganda, a pattern which underlines their status as an "urban" elite.

The non-elite Africans are also geographically mobile, but they have a different pattern of movement. Because of their low incomes, irregular employment, and the lack of a "social security" system, non-elite Africans must return periodically to their land and to their kinsmen for sustenance. By keeping a foot in both urban and rural worlds, they are also able to supplement their meager wages with subsistence farming and cash-cropping, a basic pattern for most African townsmen in Uganda and elsewhere (see Elkan 1967). Thus, when the non-elite Africans move into and out of Mbale, they usually go back and forth from their natal homes, rather than to other towns. Correspondingly, although a majority (67 percent) of the non-elite Africans have worked only in Mbale or one other town, they live there for short periods of time—almost 60 percent have been in town for less than five years. The migration of non-elite Africans is primarily between town and country, and contrasts with the circulation of elite Africans, primarily from town to town.

This pattern of geographical mobility is fairly typical of non-elite Africans in Uganda. The Sofers report that in the early 1950's more than 80 percent of the non-elite Africans in Jinja had lived there for less than five years and that 57 percent had lived there for less than two years (Sofer and Sofer 1955: 19). Southall and Gutkind, in their survey of non-elite Africans in two sections of greater Kampala, record similar statistics (Southall and Gutkind 1956:29, 251). Even Parkin, doing research in Kampala ten years later and with a relatively more stable population of informants, notes that the average length of their total residence was six to seven years (Parkin 1969:26).

The non-elite Africans also move around within Mbale as well as between Mbale and their natal homes. Since the housing of most non-elite Africans in Mbale is not a perquisite of their jobs, they are more free than elite Africans to change residence in the town. They do so for a number of reasons: the loss of a job and the related inability to pay rent; a quarrel with fellow lodgers, landlord, or neighbors; a violation of custom or law and a flight from sanctions; a desire to move closer to a friend or fellow tribesman. One of their more enterprising motives, however, is to avoid paying taxes, those of both the Mbale Municipal Council and their home districts. By adroitly moving from one part of Mbale to another or between the town and the countryside, non-elite Africans are able to avoid paying a graduated income tax (poll tax) in either place. They do this by either absenting themselves when taxes are levied or by protesting alternately to the tax collectors in one administrative unit that they have paid their taxes in the other. Finally, they are often compelled legally and politically to lead a transient existence. As indicated before, a temporary occupation license (TOL) permits a man to build on a plot of land in the undeveloped area of town either a shop, a bar, or a house; and most men build houses. However, if the Mbale Municipal Council wishes to reclaim that land, it must by law offer compensation for the buildings erected. Consequently, the town engineer's department refuses permission for anyone to build other than the most flimsy, temporary buildings. Rather than attracting a stable population, this practice undermines the residential stability of non-elite Africans.

These examples of residential changes within the town indicate that at least some of the anonymity and uncertainty of life in Mbale is purposely generated and desired by the townsmen themselves. Whatever its causes, however, the movement among both elite and non-elite Africans has the effect of undermining orderly social interaction. It isolates townsmen from one another, thereby creating obstacles to the formation and maintenance of their social relationships. Fleeting relationships are, however, a typical problem of urbanism, and Africans in Mbale deal with them in a not untypical way.

CHAPTER THREE

Social Classes

Africans in Mbale confine their friendships to their separate social worlds. The boundaries of these worlds, therefore, provide a context for the analysis of friendship behavior. Of these boundaries, the most important is that of social class, which is evident both in what people say and in what they do. The values, beliefs, and norms about social stratification, as well as the behavior of the upper-class Africans separate them from lower-class Africans and are consistent with the socio-economic differences that divide these two groups.

A Folk Model of Social Classes

Elite Africans talk about two classes of African townsmen. They label these classes in different ways: "higher" or "upper class" and "lower class," the "educated" and the "uneducated," the "big people" and the "porters," and they describe them in interactional terms. The statements of upper-class informants illustrate their beliefs about the separation between the classes:

> There are classes in Mbale, but they don't mix. The lower-class man moves with his own people, his fellow tribesmen, and he fights with others. Upper-class men, the educated people, speak English, so they can get together, regardless of their tribes.

39

> People go with people from their own level. The villagers and
> housing-estate people couldn't move with people in the senior
> quarters. They couldn't keep up with them when it came to
> giving parties or going to bars.

These comments conceptualize differences in life-style and
leisure-time behavior which elite Africans believe characterize
the two classes. Furthermore, they indicate which socio-economic attributes elite Africans think separate them from other
Africans in Mbale.

Of these different attributes, upper-class Africans attach
special significance to formal education. It provides an idiom
in which they distinguish themselves from "uneducated" non-
elite Africans. In their view it also legitimates elite status,
which becomes apparent where there is an inconsistency between upper-class status and educational achievement. As one
informant suggested:

> Those in the [government's] higher salary scale are upper class.
> But you have people in that class who are not well educated.
> There are some police officers who have only a junior secondary
> school education, and they don't fit.

The importance of education as a basis of legitimacy is further
evident in another informant's interpretation of what he
describes as a discrepancy between superior education and
subordinate position:

> The upper class are those with big jobs in the government, all
> regional and district officers. The junior officers are often better
> educated than some of the senior officers, but get less money.
> It doesn't seem right.

Their views reinforce one another. One believes that wealth
ought to be accompanied by high educational achievement, the
other, that a superior education ought to insure a higher ranking position and greater wealth.

The discrepancies which some men resent follow from the
fact that they are essentially a "new" elite. They hold senior
positions in the bureaucracies of government, in which recruit-

ment and advancement are based largely on high educational qualification. Most of these jobs first became available to Africans in the late 1950's and early 1960's when the colonial administration, in anticipation of independence, began withdrawing its expatriate officers, thereby creating high-level openings. Prior to that, Africans could get no further than the lower echelons, and that they did on a junior secondary school education and long years of loyal service. Thus, the openings which independence created were first filled by older but less educated men who had seniority. Moreover, until recently, there were few highly educated Africans available to fill those positions. Educational opportunities for Africans were quite limited until the rapid expansion of secondary school instruction which began in the 1950's. In 1948, only 84 African students completed the examinations which come at the end of secondary school training. One year less than a decade later, that number had increased almost six-fold (Goldthorpe 1965:5) and by 1961, it had grown almost eight-fold (Hunter 1963:11). Today, the young university graduate who enters the civil service often begins as an assistant to an older but considerably less educated administrator.

To say that they are a new elite, however, does not mean that they are unrelated to traditional elites, that is, to the influential men in the "tribal" society. The fathers of 23 percent of the new elite men held or hold the rank of "chief" in one of the higher administrative units (county or sub-county) into which Uganda is divided. The fathers of another 19 percent were lower level chiefs. Another 22 percent of the fathers of the new elite men were themselves employed by the protectorate administration in skilled jobs such as medical and clerical assistants or were clergymen and teachers. The fathers of the others (36 percent) were subsistence level cultivators or pastoralists. Similarly, the wives of the present elite men, though generally not as well-educated as their husbands, are the daughters of traditional elites, again mostly higher ranking chiefs.

Furthermore, at least in the beginning of their careers, some of their behavior is influenced by the fact that they are essentially the first generation of the new elite. For example, although most of them were married in church and their spouses were not chosen for them by their families, they still went through traditional ceremonies as well. One elite informant who first met his wife (J) in England where they were both students described his marriage:

We were married in church, and there were two hundred guests at a 'western style' reception afterwards. I had to foot the bill for that myself and I am economizing for it. But before the church wedding, I went to see her father to pay him bride wealth. I also had to pay for that by myself, because my father said to me when I was young that since he was paying my school fees that he wouldn't be able to pay for my bride wealth. [I asked him how he decided on the amount to pay. Here follows his description of the initial stages of the exchange.]

I got a team together to go to J's father's house to talk about the marriage. My father, his brother, my cousin [his father's brother's son], and myself. My cousin was the spokesman. I didn't say anything, and I'm not supposed to do any bargaining, nor is my father, only my spokesman. So we went to be introduced.

J's father also had a team. Besides the father there was his eldest brother, who was too old to say anything, another uncle, and J's brother, who would become my brother-in-law. We went to J's house and entered. We sat on one side and they sat on the other side. J was outside with a whole group of women from the area, and she came in to introduce me, though she didn't speak, a girlfriend of hers did. She said 'this is A.N., the District Educational Officer.'[1] At this point there was a lot of clapping and yelling from the women sitting outside. Then J was asked by her uncle if she knows me, so that she wouldn't be surprised about the marriage talk, and she said yes and for how long—in the U.K. Then J left and sat outside the house. Then J's uncle began by welcoming us and asking what we wanted. My spokesman then answered, as though he wanted to marry J instead of me, 'It's very cold at night and I have been looking for a warm blanket and I have seen a beautiful one in this house and I have come to get it.' The uncle then said, 'That is good and well spoken. The blanket is beautiful. It has many decorations.'

---

[1] I have changed the informant's occupation to preserve his anonymity.

That means that J had been to school and the U.K. The uncle continued, 'I will be very sorry to see it go, and I think you should contribute towards its decorations, since you are taking it away and I may never see it again.' My spokesman said, 'Agreed. What is the contribution?' Her uncle said, '2,500/=' [$350]. I was shocked by that figure. I expected about 1,000/= [$140]. J, who was sitting outside, yelled in, 'Father, do not sell me. My husband needs the money to begin life with.' Then my spokesman said to the uncle, 'That is well spoken. We have come here to discuss the contribution and I hope that we can speak at leisure and reach a compromise. 2,500/= is very much, I would like to contribute 800/= [$112].' The uncle said, 'Well, you have come here and we will discuss: 2,000/= [$280].' My spokesman said, 'I am glad to see that you have come down, and we will go up: 1,000/= [$140].' The uncle said, 'Well spoken, and I am glad that you have come up; we will come down: 1,500/= [$210].' My spokesman replied, 'Well spoken.' Well, I was prepared to pay 1,000/=, so I leaned over to my spokesman and said, what's 200 more shillings, go to 1,200/= [$168]. My spokesman turned to the uncle, 'We will go up to 1,200/=.' The uncle said, 'Well spoken, you have come up 1,200/= is agreed.' Then we all had a feast and drank. [Did you pay then?] No. Even if I had it then, I wouldn't have paid for it. J's family now knew me, but my family had to meet hers. Later they came to my house, had a feast, and were presented with the money.

Although this man went through a traditional marriage custom, it does not mean that he feels tied to other traditional customs nor bound to return to village life. In another discussion the same informant said, in response to my question of whether he would retire to a village or stay in some town, "I couldn't go back to a village, though I would like to get some land just outside a town, where I would be close enough to get its facilities and services. Right now, I am looking at some land where I wouldn't have to pay ground rents, premia, and other town taxes, but where I could bring in water and electricity." As will be seen, this intention to remain a townsman and not to return to the land characterizes the elite and separates them from non-elite Africans.

Notwithstanding their ties with rural kin, and perhaps because of them, elite urban Africans clearly distinguish themselves from the traditional elite. Further indication of both the

importance of education in the class concepts of elite Africans
and of their status as a new urban elite is manifest in their
discussion of differences between elite status in towns and
elsewhere. They say that in Mbale recruitment into upper-
class jobs is based on educational achievement, although "big
men" in the villages may be uneducated. One informant con-
trasted elite status in urban and rural areas:

> To village people the chief is important, but to town people, the
> chief is unimportant. In town, the educated man is more impor-
> tant. It's his education which makes him respected.

Upper-class Africans see income as another important at-
tribute of social stratification. They describe it as a means to
a life style which connotes elite status. As one informant re-
marked:

> People only meet with others who can afford to do the same
> things, or who have the same interests. Differences in income
> are basic in choosing friends.

Another man made the same point in a different way:

> Upper-class Africans don't think about income, though it is
> important. When people drink, if a man is known not to have
> money, his friends will buy for him. But he has to return the
> drinks sometime. If he doesn't, or won't be able to in the future,
> those people will stop buying for him.

These men think wealth is important for elite status because
it provides the means for sustaining reciprocity, which, as will
be discussed in more detail in Chapter Four, is itself a most
significant feature in the elite Africans' views of social stratification.

The divergent life styles which their different incomes
allow them to pursue are indicated in the household budgets
of elite and non-elite Africans. Elite Africans, for example,
spend approximately five times as much as non-elite Africans
do on both food and leisure-time activities (see Tables 1 and

2).[2] Moreover, a non-elite African who earns less than $336 per year, and 75 percent of all male adult African workers in Mbale earn less than that amount, spends his money on rent, food, and remittances to kin. Anything he spends on leisure-time activities must be deducted from the amount he has to spend on those items. He does try to reduce his expenses by going home every week, if he is able to and can afford the fare, to get plantains and other food staples (maize meal, cassava, millet, or yams) from his garden. Even then he is unable to cut his costs on items such as paraffin, charcoal, tea, sugar, milk, and any bits of fish and meat which he adds as relish to his meals. The details of the upper- and lower-class budgets are also interesting in other ways, as will be seen. Here it can be noted that upper- and lower-class Africans give to their kinsmen about the same amount of money in absolute terms, but that elite Africans give a much smaller proportion of their cash incomes. Correspondingly, upper-class Africans spend approximately 5 percent of their incomes on life insurance policies which on their retirement will pay a monthly sum that in

---

[2]The budgets included in Tables 1 and 2 are typical of those I collected. Elite informants filled out questionnaires on family income and expenditures; the forms asked, in addition to information about marital status and family size, the respondent's yearly income and monthly expenses. In many cases the details are based on estimates, and, although they seem reasonable to me and are consistent with other facts, I was unable to collect the data necessary to verify them. There are, accordingly, certain problems in the data: only one of the elite budgets shown includes an amount for taxes, although it is possible that the others either paid their taxes at one time, taking the total sum out of their savings or reduced other expenses in order to meet tax payments. Similarly, they did not include the costs of clothing or other items not usually purchased frequently or regularly. Non-elite informants gave their answers directly to an interviewer, but again they are estimates as to what they spend—none of the non-elite informants indicated paying taxes and none kept a budget for his own purposes, as did many of the elite Africans. As in the case of the elite Africans, I was unable to collect the data necessary to verify their estimates, although they also seem to be in line with the cost figures for housing, food, paraffin, and charcoal, which I was able to get independently of their accounts.

Table 1. Elite Household Income and Expenditures Per Month

	A $2452/yr. $204/mo. married; 3 children	B $2492/yr. $207/mo. married; 2 children	C $2800/yr. $233/mo. married; 4 children	D $3015/yr. $251/mo. married; 4 children	E $3268/yr. $272/mo. married; 4 children	F $3600/yr. $300/mo. married; 5 children
Rent	14.00	14.00	14.00	14.00	14.00	14.00
Utilities	11.20	11.50	10.00	17.50	9.00	20.00
Food/Household[a]	48.00	70.00	58.00	60.00	54.00	70.00
Car Installments	62.80	45.00	48.00	52.50	49.00	70.00
Car Gas and Maintenance	Reimbursed[b]	Reimbursed[b]	45.00	Reimbursed[b]	49.00	60.00
Car Insurance	21.00	14.00	7.00	14.00	14.00	7.00
Life Insurance	10.00	9.50	12.00	14.00	13.00	50.00
Kin Remittances	—	—	7.00	10.00	11.00	7.00
School Fees	11.00	13.00	9.00	9.00	8.00	15.00
Taxes	?	?	?	7.00	?	?
Savings	—	—	—	25.00	10.00	17.00
Leisure-Time Activities	26.00	30.00	23.00	28.00	41.00	40.00

[a]Includes dry cleaning and other incidentals

[b]Reimbursed by employer

Table 2. Non-Elite Household Income and Expenditures

	A $384/yr. $32/mo. married; 5 children	B $420/yr. $35/mo. married; 2 children	C $576/yr. $48/mo. married; 4 children
Rent	4.20	4.20	8.40
Utilities	—	—	—
Food/Household[a]	17.30	14.80	20.10
Car Installment	—	—	—
Car Gas and Maintenance	—	—	—
Car Insurance	—	—	—
Life Insurance	—	—	—
Kin Remittances	7.00	3.00	10.00
School Fees	—	—	2.00
Taxes	?	?	?
Savings	—	—	—
Leisure-Time Activities	3.50	8.00	7.50

[a]Includes paraffin, charcoal, and other incidentals

part will enable them to remain financially independent of their kin.

Wealth alone, however, does not justify elite status. Upper-class Africans say that educational achievement and financial success should be combined, and they do not include wealthy but uneducated Africans within their ranks. Goldthorpe noted this pattern in his general survey of elite Africans in Uganda (Goldthorpe 1965:21), and in Mbale, one informant said:

> There are very few wealthy self-employed Africans in Mbale. M is the only one I can think of, but he is uneducated and doesn't move with the civil servants, who are all educated.

In this view, as in those of other upper-class informants, elite status is confirmed by interaction with social equals, and equality is not judged on the basis of income alone.

Upper-class Africans see occupation as the link between education and income. They characterize themselves and others in terms of their jobs, as often as they do by educational levels. Indeed, in their conversations, the two are interchangeable. For example, non-elite status is exemplified by the label "porters," while elite status is typified by that of "civil servants."

In contrast to education, occupation, and income, upper-class Africans do not claim that ethnicity, or tribal identity, is a basis for elite status. This is evident in their comments about the interactional dimension of social stratification, as indicated above: they say that upper-class Africans are "educated" and "can get together regardless of their tribes." It is also indicated in the way they describe themselves: in all their descriptions of an African upper class, no informant qualified elite status by a tribal adjective. They speak of an African upper class, not of a Ganda elite, an Acholi elite, or a Gisu elite.

Their use of English is related to both the importance they attach to education and to the unimportance they ascribe to tribal identity. Upper-class informants state that their use of a common language, English, is significant to the division between themselves and other Africans:

> We can't talk to porters because they want to speak their own
> language and they don't know English.

It is noteworthy that the porters' "own language" is often the
same as an elite African's mother tongue. Saying that lower-
class Africans "want" to speak their own languages detracts
from the fact that elite Africans choose not to speak with them,
even when otherwise possible. Elite Africans speak English
both in work contexts, where it is required by their duties, and
in leisure-time situations, when they choose to use it as a sign
of elite status and as a way of talking with elite Africans from
tribal backgrounds different than their own.

Although upper-class Africans include socio-economic attributes in their standard of elite status, they view contrasting
life styles as certain indicators of social class differences. Of
particular significance to them are the political events people
follow. They say, for example, that lower-class Africans are
only interested in and talk about parochial issues, such as
neighborhood scandals and local events, whereas they follow
national and international politics. In fact, the major topics of
conversation among elite Africans in 1965-66 were Rhodesia's
unilateral declaration of independence and Britain's failure to
respond to it militaristically, the overthrow of Nkrumah in
Ghana, and the "Obote revolution" in Uganda. Non-elite Africans were concerned about the latter event, but did not talk
about international politics.

The elite also interpret differences in aspirations as evidence of the line which separates the two classes. One man
summarized these differences: "The big people want education
and the poor want land." Another informant said:

> The major differences between the big people and the porters is
> what they want: education for the educated, a piece of land for
> the peasants.

A third informant expanded on this theme:

> To the upper class, education is most important. Villagers want
> a house and land, because they know they won't be able to
> afford an education for their children and want the income from

the land. Also, without education, their children must have a place to go. The people on the housing estates think they have enough education, and they don't place much importance on it. For them, land is important as a source of income, which they think will make them more like the upper class.

The statements of these informants indicate fairly accurately what many elite Africans in fact say are their priorities: almost 50 percent said that educating their children was most important, but only 10 percent place this emphasis on acquiring land. Their beliefs about what other Africans want fit less well with the facts: 33 percent of the lower-class Africans did place first importance on land, but an equal number attached highest priority to educating their children.

Upper-class Africans frequently use modes of personal conduct as indices of social class position. For example, they say that class differences are expressed in the patterns of interaction within each class:

> I think that the lower class people are more interdependent and they can more easily beg from one another. Upper-class people are more independent, and I would never borrow anything. We are more restrained, and people are more sensitive to others' privacy.

His evaluation of the two classes is clear in his characterization of informal exchange: he refers to "begging" among lower-class Africans, but to "borrowing" among elite Africans.

Elite Africans also feel superior to non-elite Africans. Their comments about class differences and drinking customs express this attitude. One man, for example, describes what he referred to as the "subjective" side of social stratification:

> Not everyone goes to all bars. I don't go to Friends or Rafiki [bars], because the people there sing along with the jukebox. And besides, I would feel uncomfortable at Friends, and the chaps who drink there would feel uncomfortable at the Elgon Hotel [an elite bar].

His assumption that elite and non-elite Africans would "feel uncomfortable" with one another underlines the social distance which upper-class Africans perceive between themselves and other African townsmen. Other informants express this

same attitude in terms of expected discomfort and feelings of
superiority and inferiority between the classes:

> The classes in Mbale don't mix because they don't feel comfort-
> able with each other. They don't talk about the same things or
> in the same way.
> People group together by status. Feelings between the classes
> are not the same. They don't visit each other, don't keep com-
> pany. The lower class feels inferior.

This attitude of superiority on the part of elite Africans was
also noted some fifteen years earlier by the Sofers in their study
of Jinja township. They record that among the African townsmen they surveyed, an emerging elite felt so superior to lower-
class Africans as almost not to be of the same race (Sofer and
Sofer 1955:69). It is unlikely that in today's independent
Uganda any elite African would declare himself a "black European," but the basic sense of superiority appears to be similar.

The elite Africans' thoughts about the subjective aspects
of the social distance between social classes are related to their
ideas about the lack of leisure-time interaction between them.
Upper-class Africans, as described above, characterize people
in terms of the bars and dance halls they go to and in terms of
the ways in which they behave in these public places. One
informant describes different bars and drinking patterns which
he associates with elite and non-elite Africans:

> The upper-class people drink at the Elgon and Jimmy's. The
> others drink at Kikuyus, Friends, Rafiki, and Lumumba. They
> don't mix because they behave differently. The lower-class
> types like loud music, yelling, shouting, and fighting over
> women. We talk quietly and drink slowly.

Another informant makes similar distinctions:

> Saldanha's, Jimmy's, and the BCU are not bad to go to. The
> other places are too noisy, tough, and the people who go there
> are wild. That's where people throw bottles and have knife
> fights.

The elite Africans' correlation of class status and bars frequented is consistent with actual practice. Most upper-class Africans patronize four bars in Mbale: Jimmy's, Saldanha's, the "BCU" (housed in the Bugisu Co-operative Union building) and the bar in the Mt. Elgon Hotel, located in the upper-class residential area (see Plates 11 and 12). Non-elite Africans prefer different bars: Maluku, Rafiki, Friends, Lumumba, Kiteso, Kikuyu, and other smaller places located in the rural areas of town (see Plates 13 and 14).

The two sets of bars frequented by the two classes also differ physically and legally. The sharpest contrast is between bars in the developed part of Mbale and those elsewhere in the town. For example, in the rural areas a bar will often be a room in someone's mud and wattle hut, and by law it is allowed to serve only "native" beer (made from either corn, bananas, or millet). Within the center of town, the bars all look similar, being glass-fronted stores with either one or two rooms, but they differ in the number of patrons they try to accommodate. For example, two elite bars, Jimmy's and Saldanah's, each have six tables with about four chairs to a table, and twelve bar stools. In two non-elite bars, Friends and Maluku, with about the same area of floor space as the two elite bars, the former has nineteen tables, forty-one chairs, eight bar stools, and the latter has thirteen tables, thirty-eight chairs, and seven bar stools. In fact, as elite Africans contend, the non-elite bars are more crowded and are noisier.

The elite Africans' idea that lower-class people are noisy and that upper-class people are quiet is a central theme in their conceptualization of social class differences. It is manifest in their beliefs that educated people are more reserved than the uneducated and that lower-class men of different tribes only fight with one another, in contrast to the tribally heterogeneous elite who get along well together. These elements are interrelated: the educated speak a common language which they sometimes give as a "reason" for their "quietness." They are reserved in their public behavior, and they are united among themselves, despite their ethnic differences.

Thus, the statements of upper-class Africans express their view of the division, along several dimensions, between the

Plate 11. Elite Bar (BCU)

Plate 12. Elite Bar (Jimmy's)

Plate 13. Non-elite Bar (Maluku)

Plate 14. Non-elite Townsmen outside Maluku Bar

two classes of African townsmen in Mbale. They distinguish each class by differences in education, occupation, income, use of English, and other aspects of life style. Indeed, they commonly speak of the division in interactional terms. Moreover, they think of themselves as distinct and solidary; they are aware of themselves as a social class. However, their ideas, which constitute their folk model of social stratification, are based on a combination of received knowledge, preferences, and normative understandings. In fact, their folk model is relatively accurate and is extremely useful to the observer unfamiliar with actual practices, as a guide to further empirical enquiry. The degree to which the folk model is a valid representation may be seen in the interactional divisions between the two classes.

Social Classes and Interactional Boundaries

The actual behavior of upper-class Africans is consistent with their folk model of social stratification; the interactional boundaries of their system of social relations correlate with their beliefs about them. Elite Africans do interact with non-elite Africans in work tasks, but not in leisure-time activities. They also interact with non elite kinsmen, but not frequently and only then in specific, not diffuse, relationships. Furthermore, their interaction with non-Africans, Asians and Europeans, is also generally limited to occupational situations. Limited interaction, then, with both non-elite Africans and elite non-Africans circumscribes the social boundaries of the African upper class.

Elite and non-elite Africans work together, but they do not usually interact with one another in their leisure time. Leisure-time interaction here means not only that which takes place outside work hours, but also that which occurs during the work day but which does not primarily serve or promote economic ends or any other business, "functional," purpose. For example, office visiting which is not directly related to official matters or which is not regulated by economic or occu-

pational roles is considered part of leisure-time interaction. In
Mbale, elite Africans come into contact daily with non-elite
Africans, but the relationship between them is one of superior
and subordinate and is generally characterized by formal attitudes and behavior, consistent with the inequalities of their
positions. They do not engage in informal "small-talk" with
porters, office boys, messengers, and others who constitute the
lower class, although I did not observe the curtness that Goldthorpe mentions as sometimes marking the behavior of elite
Africans towards non-elite Africans (Goldthorpe 1965:77).
Lower-class Africans initiate interaction upwards only in their
specific work duties. This lack of communication outside instrumental lines is particularly evident at coffee-breaks and
other social encounters which relieve the work routine.

The social distance between elite and non-elite co-workers in the same office contrasts sharply with the informal visiting and conversation between elite colleagues from the same
office and even from different departments. Most of the central
government's regional and district offices are located in a mul-
tiple building complex at one end of Mbale's "downtown"
area, across the street from the offices of the Mbale Municipal
Council and the Bugisu Co-operative Union. Most of the
offices face out on to shaded verandas and their doors are kept
open during the day to help cool them. This also facilitates the
informal communication between colleagues. Men going from
one office to another look in on friends who work in other
offices, either stopping to chat briefly or at least to offer greet-
ings. At coffee-breaks, which elite Africans working in these
buildings often take across the street at the Bugisu Co-operative Union's coffee shop/bar, men will join friends they see
passing by their offices. In all this easy coming and going, the
elite's comraderie does not include non-elite Africans.

Elite Africans also employ non-elite Africans as
household servants, but they do not associate with them in
leisure-time activities. The wives of elite Africans, who are at
home for most of the day, occasionally get neighborhood news
from "house girls" or the wives of "house boys," and sometimes may be seen chatting with them. But even this is not
usually done in the company of the wives of other upper-class
Africans.

Elite Africans do see their non-elite kinsmen in town, but not frequently and usually not if they can avoid them. Kinship obligations connect kinsmen in the two classes, but upper-class Africans do not always acknowledge or meet these duties. They assist their poorer relatives, but with reluctance. For example, I was with an upper-class informant when he was confronted by a kinsman. It was late afternoon and we were riding in his car on one of the town's main avenues, when a shabbily dressed man rushed into the street and wildly flagged us down. At first I thought there had been an accident and that someone was in desperate need of help. My informant did not respond with any urgency, but rather slowed the car to a halt, muttering to himself. Just as the man reached the car, my informant turned to me and asked, "Does this ever happen in your country?" The pedestrian was a distant relative (a clan brother) who had come into town for the day and who was now on his way home, some 40 miles from Mbale. He had seen the car, waved it to stop, and wanted to be driven home. My informant refused, argued, and then agreed only to drop him off at the bus depot, from where he was to get home on his own. After we let him off, my informant complained that his kinsmen were always demanding too much, that he was going to cut himself off from them, and that the next time he would not even stop. Another informant, when asked about his relatives coming to him for financial help, said that he did not allow it to become a burden,

> because if they want too much or ask unnecessarily, I don't give it to them. Then they don't come back. They may not care for me anymore, but I don't care what they will say about me.

The elite Africans described by Goldthorpe also had a problem dealing with their uneducated kinsmen. He mentions that they grumbled about how much financial help they were expected to give to their poorer relatives, although he also notes that they tended to comply with such requests. Indeed, Goldthorpe estimates that some men gave cheerfully, that most men gave reluctantly, and that a few others rebelled and refused altogether (*Ibid.*, 76). Although I do not have much quantitative data on this issue for the elite Africans in Mbale, it is my impression that most men still give reluctantly, but that the other proportions have been reversed: a few give cheerfully and some do not give at all.

The nature of their contact with non-elite kinsmen is also exemplified in a kind of "structural amnesia," a process more commonly described in the manipulation of genealogical relationships (see Bohannan 1952). Not only do upper-class Africans refuse the requests of their lower-class kinsmen, but they sometimes manage to "forget" their ties with them. For example, one informant, when asked if he had any kinsmen in Mbale, first gave two names, and then later after the question was repeated, mentioned as an afterthought, a third name. The kin who was thus added was a porter, and the others who were first mentioned were of elite status. Furthermore, this informant said that he visited "socially" with the first two, but not with the other. Thus, although there is interaction between relatives in the two classes, the upper-class Africans limit its nature and its frequency. As a result, relationships between elite and non-elite kinsmen are similar to that between superior and subordinate in the functional tasks of the work situation.

Elite Africans explain their indifference towards and lack of interaction with non-elite kinsmen in terms of their own independence from home affairs. They contend that kinsmen were traditionally bound to one another because people often needed help in their daily activities and that they exchanged goods and services with relatives who were also neighbors. But in town such exchanges are unnecessary, because, from their point of view, they are economically independent. Furthermore, they say that maintaining good relations with relatives would be necessary if one wanted to claim land in one's home area. However, they explain that they have alternatives to returning to their tribal homes, since they can buy land elsewhere, particularly in and around Uganda's urban centers. Thus, when the obligations of kinship become too onerous, they would rather risk not being welcomed home than to meet their relatives' demands.

To what extent they refuse requests from non-elite kinsmen and do not go home is empirically an open question. They do send money to poor relatives (see Table 1), and some will house a niece or nephew who is going to secondary school in Mbale. But because they are a new urban elite in Uganda, there was little opportunity to test their assertions that they were not going back to village life. During the field-work period no one retired and none quit their jobs except to join other urban-based companies. Many said they were buying land in or near urban areas, as exemplified in the informant's statements quoted above. Another informant, a young man, said that his parents were nagging him because, although he could afford it, he had not built a house in his home village. Moreover, he said that he did not visit them very often because they nagged him and because he had no intention of building a house there nor of returning home. Whether these new elite Africans retire to life in a town or in a village and what role they play in urban or rural affairs after they leave their jobs are questions for further research.

Upper-class Africans have contact with Asians and Europeans, but also only in specific and limited circumstances. Their interaction with non-African colleagues tends to be centered around work tasks. They sometimes associate with Asian businessmen, but such relationships are instrumental in character. In many of these cases, the Asians attempt to secure the "goodwill" of African civil servants who deal with licensing procedures and other rules of public order. However, upper-class Africans do not claim friendship with Asians. Furthermore, elite Africans do not mix socially with the Europeans in Mbale. Some elite Africans belong to a social club in town which has a predominantly European and Asian membership, but they primarily use its athletic facilities and generally do not drink at the club's bar. It is my impression that the absence of informal interaction between the elite Africans and the elite non-Africans in Mbale reflected their mutual lack of interest in one another. This is, in turn, consistent with my impression that in Mbale non-Africans of elite status appear to be less cosmopolitan than those in Kampala, where elite Africans do have friends among non-Africans, usually Europeans rather than Asians (see Kumalo 1966:218-219, Southall 1966:351). It also reflects, as will be seen, the elite's values, beliefs, and norms about sociability.

CHAPTER FOUR

The Culture of Friendship

For Africans in Mbale, friendship is a haven against the anonymity and uncertainty of urban life. They value companionship, deplore loneliness, and pity the man without friends. They also suspect and avoid him, believing him to be irresponsible since he cannot be guided and constrained by his peers. Friendship, however, is not given or accepted indiscriminately; Africans of both classes restrict their friendships to those they consider social equals. Thus to understand their friendship behavior, it is essential to analyze their ideas about social equality, and the system of values, beliefs and norms of which they are a part.

Cultural Analysis

Cultural analysis is necessary for understanding their behavior, because socio-economic interpretations do not adequately account for the lack of interaction between upper- and lower-class Africans. The social distance between them is understandable only partly in terms of their different socio-economic circumstances. The differences in their incomes are critical when related to their patterns of drinking and going to bars, which are centers of friendship activities and interaction. The biggest and busiest bars in Mbale are located in the central part of town. The distance between them and the residential area of upper-class Africans is about a half-hour's walk or a few minutes' ride, and most elite Africans have cars. It is at least the same distance or even longer for most non-elite Africans to get to these bars from their homes in the rural areas, and most of them do not have cars. Furthermore, there is no public bus service within the town and taxis are irregular and relatively expensive. Many lower-class Africans have bicycles, but that mode of travel is neither convenient nor safe, particularly after dark, in getting to and from the bars.

The sort of danger which threatens non-elite Africans who live in the rural areas of Mbale or in villages outside the town's boundaries and who have to walk or bicycle into town is exemplified in a complaint contained in the "Letters to the Editor" column of the *Uganda Argus,* Uganda's English-language daily newspaper. The following letter appeared in the December 1, 1965 issue:

> For a very long time now, . . . the Mbale-Tororo Road [the main road which connects Mbale with Kampala] has proved to be a spot of terror. Very many people have been victims of beatings and have had their belongings such as bicycles etc. taken away from them. In more than one incident the victims received panga cuts and in one case a victim nearly lost his arm. All these things happen because the place after P.M. is so dark that even in a clear moonlight everybody is scared to travel across it. . . .
>
> The people who are the victims of these attacks are always either travelling to and from their work within the Municipality or travel to the town to patronize the beer bars.

In addition to these logistic constraints, the costs of drinking limit the opportunities for elite and non-elite Africans to drink together. The fifty bars in Mbale are licensed by the municipal council to sell liquor, "European" beer, or "native" beer (usually manufactured from corn, millet or plantain). The prices of these drinks vary: a bottle of European beer (50¢) costs three times as much as a bowl of native beer (14¢). None of the bars in the developed area of town sell native beer, and none of the bars scattered throughout the rural areas are licensed to sell liquor and few there sell European beer. Thus, the unavailability of the less expensive drinks in Mbale's "downtown" bars makes it impractical for non-elite Africans to drink at them and with elite Africans.

These logistic and economic factors act to constrain people's behavior, regardless of their wishes. The meager cash incomes of the lower-class Africans prohibit them from participating in the costly friendship activities of upper-class Africans; they explain why the non-elite Africans cannot and do not drink with the elite Africans. But, socio-economic factors do not explain why elite Africans, with their greater wealth, do not drink with non-elite Africans, thereby choosing to exclude them from their friendships. Rather, their behavior is understandable in terms of their ideas about friendship, and especially their ideas about reciprocity and respectability.

Friendship and Pride

To upper-class Africans, friendship means sociability. Indeed their ideal of a "good man" is often described as one who is "just" and "sociable," who has a "good circle of friends," and who "does not want to fight." They consider association with other men in leisure-time to be usual and desirable, and they contrast friendliness with being "proud," a label which they attach to those who remain alone. Their equation of separation and pride occurs in several different contexts. For example, when the Asian owner of one of the elite bars suggested hanging curtains between tables for privacy, one informant commented "it would be foolish to put up curtains. You come drinking to be with people, not to be alone." Another example is that of an upper-class family, consisting of a man, his wife, and four children who used only three of the five bedrooms in their house. When asked why his children slept in two rooms, while the other rooms went unoccupied, he explained that each child did not have his own room because "they would be lonely if they had to sleep alone" and because "living alone would be taken as a sign that they did not get along well with one another." The house, originally built by the British protectorate government for its expatriate officials with their standards of personal space and acceptable conduct, is ill-designed for the cultural conceptions of its African residents.

Their conception of friendship as sociability is also evident in other behavior. It is manifest simply in the fact that they get together with other townsmen in their leisure hours. Their short stay and limited commitments in Mbale could make tenuous the development of regular informal relationships. Furthermore, although they are in close physical proximity with one another through their work and residence, this would not necessitate the emergence of friendships. It is conceivable that they could take part in occupational and economic relationships only, without otherwise becoming involved with one another. The value which they attach to sociability, however, draws them into informal contacts, sustains their friendships, and relieves them of the burden of loneliness.

Such an emphasis on sociability, however, is not limited to either urbanites or Africans. A similar theme is described in other cultures, as well. For example, Monica Wilson's *Good Company* is a classic ethnography of a rural African people's traditional values of friendship. In it she describes the Nyakyusa's basic values of fellowship and conviviality, which they too contrast with remaining apart and being "proud" (Wilson 1951:66-90). In their account of community life among urban working-class Englishmen, Willmott and Young illustrate that friendship, with its implication of regular and frequent association with "mates," particularly in local pubs, is the standard of leisure-time conduct. Its absence is attributed by the people themselves to being "big-headed," "high and mighty," or thinking of oneself to be a "cut above everybody else" (Wilson and Young 1957:154), attitudes which African townsmen in Mbale would easily recognize and describe as signs of pride.

The significance of friendship to elite Africans in Mbale can be better seen when leisure-time companionship is viewed

in the context of their daily routine. Typically, a man's working hours are spent in his office. During the day, he has opportunities for friendship contacts primarily through coffee-break
gatherings. Most government offices, as noted before, are
located within a few blocks of each other and all are within a
few minutes' walk of the Bugisu Co-operative Union's popular
coffee shop and bar. It is common to see at the BCU, at mid-
morning and mid-afternoon of any workday, small groups of
friends sitting together and talking or reading the daily newspaper.

After work, but before dinner, which is usually about 8
P.M., a man may spend his time in a number of different ways.
He may go shopping (most men, married or single, buy the
major food items). If not shopping, he may spend time in a bar
in town talking with a few friends, or he may spend it at home
either with his family or working around the house or garden.
He may also use those hours for taking care of odd jobs, in
which he is not usually joined by friends.

In the evening, between about 7:30 and 9:30, a man will
have dinner at home. It is usual among elite Africans for adults
to dine after the children go to bed, and this is a quiet time in
which a man and his wife are able to talk over the day's events.
It is unusual to invite friends home for dinner, although meals
are shared with others on special occasions.

After dinner, a man usually meets his friends. If he is an
older man, he will meet with his friends either at his or their
homes or he will go to one of the "quieter" bars in town.
"Quietness," in the sense it is used among elite Africans,
means that the music does not blare, that there are few non-
elite Africans in the bar, and that there are fewer prostitutes.

The comparative term is appropriate because prostitutes
are found in all bars in Mbale. Many of them are local girls,
but some are "old pros" who travel the circuit of Uganda's
urban centers, and most of them work out of bars. In one bar,
for example, the girls are on display downstairs, but use the
rooms upstairs when they are with their clientele. The cus-
tomer pays for the room, and the girls get 20 shillings ($2.80)
if the man is European or from 2 to 5 shillings (28¢ to 70¢) if
the man is Asian or African. However, elite African customers

usually sit and drink with the girls, buying their drinks, and therefore they pay the equivalent of 15 to 20 shillings. The bar owner, in this case, does not get a kickback from the girls because they bring him a great deal of business.

A younger man usually goes out every night. Young men will either drive to their friends' houses and then go with them to bars in town, or more usually, they will go directly to the bars, looking for their friends. There are only a few bars in Mbale which are popular with elite Africans, and a man will go to one where he thinks his friends will be and will either meet them or wait for them there. If, after a while, he has not met a friend, he will move on to another bar; bar-hopping is not an unusual pattern and a bar which is empty at one point in the evening may be filled shortly thereafter.

Owning a car and having the cash to operate and maintain it are important factors in the social life of elite Africans and to the division between them and non-elite Africans. Most upper-class Africans have cars because they are able to buy them with loans secured from their employers, both government and private (see Table 1). Cars facilitate their "moving around" town, and they free men from interacting only with neighbors, although in Mbale most elite Africans live in one area of town. Even then, elite Africans do not choose their friends from nearby neighbors, as do most non-elite Africans.

On weekends, the pattern is similar to that during the week, except that men are likely to spend even more time in the bars. Some men will take their wives to a bar, to a dance, or to see a film, although it is usual even on weekends for men and women to have separate social lives except for special events.

It is an obvious pattern in Mbale that bars are important places of friendship activities, and there are several reasons for it. One is simply that drinking is a favorite pastime. Another is that there are few alternative places to meet. Men do not use the church halls in Mbale as meeting places because they either charge rent, prohibit drinking, or exclude bar-girls. Also, other elite Africans who stop overnight in Mbale on business trips often relax by going to the bars. The town's upper-class residents go to bars on the chance that they will find old friends among the travelers. Contributing further to the importance of bars is the fact that husbands and wives are generally expected to, and do, lead different social lives, and since it is socially accepted that the home is a woman's domain, bars offer a context in which their worlds may be kept separate.

The significance of bars as places of informal companionship is also consistent with the fact that in Mbale few upper-class Africans belong to formal groups or voluntary associations. Not being "joiners" is a pattern also reported among new elite Africans in Nigeria (Lloyd 1967:148). Less than 15 percent of them even nominally claim membership in any such organization, and those to which they belong are not tribal associations but "Old Boy" associations, service clubs (joined primarily by elite Africans working in private industry), and the civil servants association. Several factors explain their lack of participation. Their economic independence precludes any need to join the sort of mutual aid societies that lower-class Africans usually join when coming to the city, and their frequent transfers undermine the establishment of social clubs which depend on a stable population for membership and funding. These factors make Mbale's public places (bars, restaurants) especially important in its social life. Furthermore, although voluntary associations run by permanent organizations might attract some people, the only such organizations in Mbale are the churches, which do not sponsor men's clubs.

Friendship and Reciprocity

The rights and duties which elite Africans understand to be fundamental to friendship follow from their emphasis on sociability as its primary characteristic. Companionship is the major mutual claim friends can make on one another. It entails pursuing common interests, sharing experiences, and giving and receiving advice, encouragement, and sympathy, when needed. All of these exchanges are set in the context of frequent face-to-face interaction. Indeed, they expect to see one another several times a week, if not daily.

I became particularly aware of this expectation from their reactions to me when I tried to follow a field work schedule by which I could maintain systematic and regular contact with my informants. My daily routine, particularly when I was working with upper-class Africans, included a brief visit with as many informants as possible. Often, I was able to drop in at their offices for a few minutes' conversation, usually without an appointment after our first or second encounter. If I could not manage that, I tried to see them either during coffee-breaks (at the BCU), or immediately after work in the bars. If I also missed them then, I stopped off at their homes, before dinner, or tried to catch up with them after dinner, again in the bars.

This schedule worked in the early part of field work when I knew and saw only a few people. However, with the increase in the number of people and with the other leads I wanted to follow-up, I was eventually unable to maintain it. I then shifted to seeing a different set of between ten and twenty men each day of the work week, using my time in the afternoons, evenings, and on weekends, to broaden and deepen my relationships with a smaller number of informants, who had become, by then, friends. After I changed my schedule, I was able to visit with most people, and even with some of my friends, only a few times each week. That was when I learned directly about their ideas of companionship: I would walk into somebody's office or see someone on the street or in a bar that I had not seen for several days and, particularly if we were close friends, they would greet me with "You have been lost! Where have you been?" They expected that we would be in almost constant contact and that I would account for my "disappearances," just as they would tell me when they were going out of town, were not feeling well, or simply were not "moving around" town for a while.

Related to the expectation of companionship, reciprocity in drinking is perhaps the most important specific obligation of friendship among elite Africans. In accord with their understanding that to offer a drink to or to drink with someone is symbolic of friendship, their usual practice is for a set of friends either to alternate in buying rounds in an evening or for one man to buy most of the drinks at one time, to be repaid in kind at another time. In either case, men expect reciprocity and friendship would not be maintained with a man who violated that principle. This is as true of someone who receives but does not give as it is of someone who gives but does not expect or allow reciprocity. One informant said about the first case:

> You might be rich and I might be poor, and we could be friends. But since you're rich and I'm poor, you'd buy the drinks. That's acceptable sometimes, but after a while it's not, and the friendship wouldn't last, because I couldn't buy you drinks. It wouldn't have to be drink for drink, but, over time, it should be about even for friendship.

Another informant indicated, in response to a question about the political activities of Mbale's elite Africans, that an exchange unbalanced the other way was also unacceptable:

> There's very little politicking here. The reason is that there's nothing to be political about in Mbale. Of course, when a man wants something, he talks with the people, buys them drinks. Like M who wants to go to Kampala [i.e., to sit in parliament]. He tries to buy everybody, always talking, drinking.

Although informants did not explicitly contrast them, they do differentiate between the reciprocity expected in friendship and the pay-off found in patronage.

Consistent with the obligation to reciprocate in drinking behavior, the basic sanction for not meeting that responsibility or for violating any of the norms surrounding the friendship relation is the withholding of companionship. Elite Africans generally do not berate, or otherwise publicly pass verbal judgement on one another's behavior. If a man consistently does not conform to the expectations of his peers, they simply and quietly dissociate themselves from him. They do not inform him of their plans, do not include him in their activities, do not drink with him; in short, they drop him from their circle of friends. And in a situation like that in Mbale, where sociability is so highly valued and companionship requires an explicit effort of getting together socially, isolating an individual is an effective sanction on deviant behavior.

Although companionship and conviviality best typify the kind of reciprocity expected in elite friendships, friendship has other dimensions. For example, many elite Africans are required by their jobs to be on the road for short periods of time, and, when a man goes out of town, he expects that a friend will "look after" his family just as he would be expected to look after his friend's family. "Looking after" requires a man, or his wife, to be available to the other's family for lending a hand with household chores like shopping, in case of sudden illness, or for any other emergency which might arise. In fact, I observed and heard of only a few instances in which these kinds of help were necessary or called for.

Generally, elite Africans do not expect money or other kinds of economic assistance from their friends. Their incomes from their jobs and other investments preclude their financial dependence on others in ordinary matters. Also, they say that if they needed to borrow money, they would use the banks or credit unions. Furthermore, since elite Africans come to Mbale specifically because of a work assignment, they do not have to rely on others to support them while they hunt for a job; nor do they have a problem in finding a place to live, since assigned housing is one of the perquisites of senior service in both public and private organizations. The major consequence of this financial independence is that friendships among upper-class Africans seem to be essentially expressive in nature: theirs is a reciprocity in which economic exchange is less frequent, and to them less important, than sharing "good company."

The non-elite Africans' ideology of friendship is similar in certain respects to that of elite Africans, but it also differs significantly. The major difference is in the content of reciprocity expected of friends. Although lower-class Africans value sociability, their friendships are marked by an emphasis on the exchange of goods and services. For example, there are two friends who are carpenters and who borrow tools and other equipment from one another, and two other friends, one of whom is a butcher and the other a vegetable seller, who regularly trade food stuffs.

The same theme appears in their work-based friendships. Occupational contacts are important in the friendships of all Africans who work in Mbale but they mean different things in the two classes. Most of the elite Africans are bureaucrats, so their work in Mbale does not involve the cultivation of a patron-client type of relationship as a basis for financial success; thus their friendships derived from the work situation are not particularly instrumental in character. Many of the non-elite Africans are craftsmen or petty traders, so friendships based on occupational contacts are linked to the development and maintenance of a market-type relationship; the idea of economic exchange is common in their comments about their friends:

> My friend sells fish. I bought from him, and we established our friendship in that way.

> My friend has a local shop, and we have become so friendly, that he gives me things on credit.

Besides these instances, other forms of economic exchange, though irregular, are important in non-elite friendships. When a man comes to town, he looks for a relative or friend to stay with until he can find or afford a place of his own. If a man loses his job, he expects to be able to, and in practice does, move in with a friend. And if a man needs money to meet his daily expenses, which is not unusual among non-elite Africans in the town, he expects a friend to help him. In fact, when a lower-class African is asked what he can expect from a friend his answer is, first and foremost, financial assistance in contrast to the elite African's companionship.

Friendship and Respectability

Elite Africans consider men social equals if they are able to comply with the reciprocity expected in friendship. Reciprocity, however, is only one of two major ideas which underlie their interpretation of social equality. The other is contained in the axiom that friends should be "respectable" men. To them, respectability is achieved by meeting one's obligations, including those of friendship and those of domestic life, which are, for a man, primarily keeping his family well-fed and clothed and providing for the education of his children. Only those who meet these obligations at the same time that they meet the obligations of friendship are considered respectable. Their concept of respectability necessitates maintaining a balance between different obligations, and they describe not maintaining such a balance as "excessive" behavior, which they consider disreputable.

While excessive behavior means failure to strike a balance between the obligations of friendship and those of domestic life, elite Africans do not define excessive behavior absolutely. Rather, they judge behavior to be excessive in relation to one's status, which implies one's financial resources. For example, they say that it is not necessarily wrong for a man to drink every day as long as he does not go into debt or spend the money which he would otherwise use to buy food and clothing for his family or to pay school fees for his children. Therefore, an elite African who drinks frequently but who is able to meet his other obligations to provide for his family is not considered excessive. A non-elite African who spends the same amount of money drinking will be unable to provide for his family and is consequently thought by elite Africans to be excessive. Their rejection of non-elite Africans as friends because of their alleged excessive behavior is thus an integral part of elite friendship culture and is consistent with the socio-economic differences between the two classes. Non-elite Africans are precluded from elite friendships not only because they ordinarily cannot meet the high costs of drinking which these relationships demand, but because even if they did so, elite Africans would claim that then they could not be meeting other domestic obligations and thus were excessive and disreputable.

Similarly, the idea of balancing friendship obligations and domestic responsibilities throws light on a pattern of interaction among elite Africans themselves. Elite Africans often describe a man's age in terms of domestic obligations: a man who is expected to provide for the welfare of a wife and children is considered an "older" man; one who has no such responsibilities is considered a "younger" man. Thus, they do not judge a young man's actions to be excessive if he drinks often, goes to dances, and has many girlfriends. They condemn the same behavior in an older man, not because those activities themselves are thought disreputable but because it is assumed that such a man may not be meeting his other obligations. It is a question of balancing the costs of friendship and the costs of supporting a family.

The elite Africans' lack of informal interaction with non-Africans is also understandable in terms of this ideology. Just as it is excessive to go out drinking too often, to stay at home too often and not to join in the conviviality of friendship would tip the scale the other way and would be condemned as excessive behavior. The elite Africans say that a man who spends too much time at home is "proud" and unfriendly. And since non-African men spend much of their leisure-time at home, they are thought to be unfriendly, regardless of other interpretations which they may place on their own behavior. One informant made this point when discussing how money should be spent:

> If you spend all your money on drinks and girls, then you won't have any for a home. But if you don't go out to bars, people will think you're not sociable, and that's bad. Even if you have the biggest house and you sit in it all day all by yourself, then people will think you're proud. They'll say you're an *mzungu* [European], hopeless.

Although they evaluate a man's sociability and his pride in terms of the ratio of time he spends with his friends and at home, they temper their judgement with respect to a man's domestic responsibilities: they expect younger men to be out with friends more often than older men who they think ought to spend more time with their families at home.

This ideology is also evident in the behavior of the wives of elite Africans. Among these women, friendship primarily entails visiting in one another's homes, thought to be a pleasant way to spend a morning or an afternoon. However, to go out so often that a woman does not have time to meet *her* domestic obligations of caring for children and preparing or, in the case of most elite Africans, supervising the preparation of meals is said to be excessive. The expected balance, in this case, is between time spent visiting friends and time spent attending to household tasks. One example illustrates the elite wives' conception of excessive behavior. One week a group of government officials came to Mbale and several parties were given in their honor. Several wives were returning home from one such gathering and were talking about the excitement of such events. All agreed that the parties were fun, but they also expressed doubts about going to further festivities since they felt that their extended absences from home were "excessive."

The elite Africans' ideas about respectability, and their interpretation of it as a balance between obligations in different social relationships or situations, is not unique to them, and, like other elements in their culture of friendship, is found in other societies. For example, Ulf Hannerz' study (1969) of the social evaluation of different life styles in an American ghetto provides material for comparative analysis. He describes two categories of ghetto dwellers, which his informants referred to as "respectable" people and "undesirables." Furthermore, they judge respectability by relative, not absolute standards, not simply in terms of particular acts, but with reference to a balance of behavior in basic roles. The balance they have in mind is also between a man's familial responsibilities—providing his wife and children with food and clothing and spending money: "taking good care of the family" —and the obligations of "sociability" (*Ibid.*, 40, 45, 59). Indeed, if a man has an income sufficient to support the costs of his family's needs and those of his having a "good time" with friends, male or female, outside the household, then his behavior is not considered disreputable, or, in the idiom of Africans in Mbale, "excessive" (*Ibid.*, 62–63). However, they judge the same behavior, *i.e.*, spending money on drinking with friends or keeping another woman as excessive or "undesirable" if it interferes with a man's meeting his familial obligations. And in Hannerz' account, as in Mbale, "respectable" men choose as friends their social equals, avoiding association with "undesirables" (*Ibid.*, 34–36).

The parallel in ideas is even more interesting since Hannerz' informants also evaluate moral status in relation to an individual's developmental cycle. As with Africans in Mbale, the people with whom Hannerz worked adjust their interpretation of undesirable behavior in accord with a person's age, measured in terms of domestic obligations. For example, an individual who does not have to contribute money or time to a spouse or children has more resources for intensive and wide-ranging sociability. He can thus act as a "swinger" with its implication of youth regardless of his actual age. Conversely, a young person with such obligations cannot remain a "swinger" for very long. This is particularly evident in the case of unwed mothers who have to take care of their children (*Ibid.*, 60). Yet, as Hannerz notes, childbearing and childrearing do not necessarily mean that a woman's sociability will be considered excessive; if she leaves her child or children with her own mother or if she lives in her mother's household, she will be relatively free of domestic obligations and therefore will be available for sociability without stigma (*Ibid.*, 60–61). Thus, in both America and Uganda, the application of standards of conduct is relative to status differences, especially those of social class and sex, and therefore social behavior becomes fully intelligible only when viewed in its cultural context.

Friendship and Social Equality

To Africans in Mbale, then, social equals are men who conform to the reciprocity they expect in their friendships and, especially among elite Africans, who are able to do so without jeopardizing their standing as respectable men. The cultural meaning of social equality is thus based on their beliefs about reciprocity and respectability. Although these two concepts are analytically separable, they are directly related in their friendship culture. Respectability and reciprocity represent different temporal dimensions of the rights and duties of friendship; the former reflects the short-run, and the latter, the long-run aspects of the relationship. The ideal of respectability is based on successfully meeting obligations in different basic roles. It implies that a person is capable, at any given time, of honorably fulfilling the expectations which exist between friends. Reciprocity, on the other hand, implies a series of transactions, over time, between individuals who claim to be friends. This contrast underlies in part the elite African's argument that even if non-elite Africans could somehow afford to drink with them at a given time, they would still be unacceptable as friends because of their inability to reciprocate over the long-run. Thus, the principle of friendship with social equals implies that men should choose as friends those with whom they can expect a continuing, recurrent, and therefore long-run exchange.

CHAPTER FIVE

The Structure of
Friendship

Africans in Mbale choose their friends in accord with their culture of friendship. This culture is manifest first of all in the division between elite and non-elite Africans, but it is also apparent in friendships within each class. Before describing these friendship patterns, it is useful to comment on the sorts of information on which their analysis is based. One type of data follows from what informants said about friendship. Elite Africans say that friends ought to interact frequently; therefore, I used frequency of leisure-time association as a criterion for objectively identifying a man's friends. These data were compared with a second subjective kind of information: those whom informants claimed as friends. Daily observation over the field work period supported their statements about their friendships; the individuals whom a man verbally identified as friends were in fact those with whom he spent most of his free time.

The analysis of friendships, moreover, is based on the study of dyadic relationships. Pairs of friends are the analytical units, the focus of study being the relationship between two individuals and their respective socio-economic attributes. These I examined within the context of friendship sets. Most men have a few "close" friends with whom they spend more time than they do with others. I took those friends (usually between two and four) with whom a man most often interacted as the primary data to be analyzed.

Friendship among Upper-Class Africans

Within the context of their daily routine, elite Africans choose as friends those who are their social equals. This means, first of all, that they choose as friends only fellow elite Africans. No upper-class informant selects, either verbally or interactionally, a lower-class African as a friend. Through hundreds of hours of interviews and informal conversation, no elite informant ever mentioned, directly or indirectly, spending his leisure time with any men other than other elite Africans. Moreover, over thousands of observations in bars, homes, offices, and on the street, I never saw an elite African with a non-elite African in the context of friendship activity. Along both verbal and non-verbal dimensions, the friendship behavior of elite Africans was consistent with their beliefs, values, and norms of friendship.

This division in leisure-time interaction between elite and non-elite Africans is not limited to either Mbale or Uganda. A pattern of stratified friendships among African townsmen was observed in Jinja in the early 1950's (Sofer and Sofer 1955:46). There "professionals" confined their friendships to their own group, avoiding association with the "porters." The Smythes also described a division between a new urban elite and other Africans in Nigeria in the later 1950's (Smythe 1960:94–102); and Lloyd's observations in the early 1960's confirms their analysis (Lloyd 1967:146). In South Africa, as well, elite Africans are described as choosing their friends from among their social equals (Kuper 1965:99).

Within the upper class itself, friends are also chosen in accord with the principle of social equality. These are men who are in the same or similar occupations, and who are at similar points in their careers, both occupational and domestic. Thus, most elite Africans select their friends from among colleagues. Of sixty senior civil servants, 80 percent of their friends are also central government employees. And among those elite

Africans who work in local government, public corporations, and private industry, there is also a greater than proportional choice of friends from among colleagues within their own organizations than outside them. These choices are presented in Table 3.[1]

Table 3. Elite Friendship Choices Within Own or Other Occupational Organization

	Own	Other	Total Choices
Central Government (60 men)	120 (86)	30 (64)	150
Local Government (22 men)	30 (13)	31 (48)	61
Public Corporations (12 men)	9 (3)	17 (23)	26
Private Industry (11 men)	15 (3)	12 (24)	27
Total (105 men)	174 (105)	90 (159)	264

[1]In Table 3, as well as in the other tables summarizing the friendship choices among upper-class Africans, both actual and expected choices are noted in order to provide a standard against which to measure the significance of the patterns. The rationale for the two sets of numbers is that actual choices may be compared with a model in which choices are considered to be random (see Coleman 1958: 34–36 and Fararo and Sunshine 1964:7). In the model the expected number of choices within any category is the product of the proportion of people in that category and the total number of their choices. For example, the 60 central government employees, who represent 57 percent of the upper-class Africans, named 150 people as friends, and the expected number of their friends within the central government would be 86 (.57 x 150). The actual number of their friends within the central government is 120, which is statistically as well as socially significant. The expected frequency of choices is included within parentheses in these tables.

A similar pattern occurs within the central government itself. There men choose friends from among their colleagues within their own departments: men with whom they have interacted in the past and with whom they will most likely interact again in the future. This continuity of association is especially conducive to the reciprocity expected in friendship. These choices, analyzed for the four largest departments in which there are at least five men of elite status among whom choice could be exercised, are presented in Table 4.

Table 4. Elite Friendship Choices Within Own or Other Department Within Central Government

	Own	Other	Total Choices
Police (14 men)	16 (6)	10 (20)	26
Education (10 men)	19 (4)	6 (21)	25
Administration (9 men)	13 (4)	11 (20)	24
Agriculture (5 men)	7 (1)	4 (10)	11

The concept of common career can suitably be stretched to include those who went to high school together, since in Uganda attending secondary school is usually the first significant break with non-elite Africans and is the basis for recruitment into future occupations. As Goldthorpe notes, secondary schools in Uganda are actively anti-tribal and English is their medium of instruction (Goldthorpe 1965:51–52). Most of the elite Africans in Mbale have attended, at different times, one of six or seven secondary schools, which, as boarding schools, provided opportunities for meeting other men who have since become a part of the African elite in Uganda. They occasionally reminisce about "Old Boy" networks, based on having been to a particular school, for example King's College, Budo or St.

Mary's College, Kisubi (many secondary schools in Uganda have "college" in their names), although these seem to bear on friendships less than their talk would suggest. Of 55 elite Africans for whom I have the necessary data, there were 47 pairs of men who had been to school together and who could choose friends from among former schoolmates. About 40 percent of them did so. Attendance at the same secondary school does not necessarily mean that men will be friends later on, but this experience is for many elite Africans one of the first situations during their careers, away from home and on the move, in which they establish friendships which are renewed at different points in their lives.

Another kind of data that suggests the significance of common careers is the proportion of current friendships first established in other work posts. Thus, of 121 friends claimed by 41 men, only about 30 percent were first met in Mbale; the other 70 percent were first met elsewhere through work contacts, usually in the major towns of Uganda. These men know one another from their work prior to their arrival in Mbale and they can expect to renew their relationships with one another in their future assignments.

The interplay between career lines and friendship patterns is also evident when their work and friendship histories are juxtaposed. One example is A, who is employed in the central government's administrative service. He has been in Mbale for a year. Before that he had been posted in Mbarara and Jinja. One of his closest friends is B, a police officer. He first met him in Jinja, when they were both assigned there: "We met at work; you know, police and administration join forces."

Another example is C, who works for the Mbale Municipal Council and has been in Mbale for six months. Before arriving there he was an accountant in the Ugandan army for three years, during which time he was stationed in Jinja. Among his closest friends in Mbale is D, a police officer. C first met D in Jinja through his own brother, also a police officer, who had also been posted in Jinja. C's brother and D were themselves colleagues and friends. D was transferred to Mbale, and when C arrived in town, upon assuming his present position, they renewed their friendship.

E's career and friendships provides a similar example. He is an administrator in the service of the central government. He has been in Mbale for the past two years, and he worked in Entebbe and Jinja before. F, an education officer, is one of his closest friends. E first met F in Entebbe, through a mutual friend with whom E then worked. F and the mutual friend had been co-workers before that in Kampala. After E came to Mbale, F was transferred here and they resumed their friendship.

A fourth example is G, an officer in the Ministry of Labor. He was new to Mbale, having been posted there for only one month. He has worked for the central government for five years since leaving school in 1960. During that time, he has been transferred five times, spending a year each in Kampala, Masaka, Jinja, Ft. Portal, and then again in Kampala. Among his closest friends is H, an engineer who is also employed by the central government and who also has seen service in several different places in the past ten years. G first met H during his first assignment in Kampala. Although then they had not been especially close friends, they have renewed and strengthened their relationship since finding one another in Mbale.

Friendships first established in Mbale also reflect the influence of occupational contacts. For example, I is a financial officer for the Mbale Municipal Council. He has been there since 1960. J is one of his closest friends. He first met J, who works for the central government's Office of Lands and Surveys, soon after arriving in Mbale. They met on the job: they each represent their respective departments at joint meetings of local and national government. I says of J: "He was the first young person I met when I arrived in Mbale. After one meeting we went to a bar for a drink and we have become close friends since then."

Not only do work contacts influence patterns of leisure-time association, but changes in occupational circumstances are reflected in the interaction between friends. This can be seen in the process whereby a man who arrives in Mbale without friends from former experiences becomes acclimated to his new situation. For example, I first saw K the day after he arrived in Mbale. This was his first assignment upon entering the civil service, and he knew no one in the town. When I interviewed him again one month after his arrival, he said that he had become friends with the two men with whom he shared an office. He also mentioned meeting others around town through these new friends, but that his colleagues were his closest companions.

The influence of a change in work status can also be seen when there are personnel shifts in the offices with which a man's work brings him into contact, although his own position remains constant. An example of this situation centers on L, an agricultural officer in charge of one of the districts neighboring on Mbale. When first interviewed, L named as his friends M, an administrative officer for that same district, N, a departmental colleague, and O, who worked for the co-operative which processed and sold a major cash-crop grown in that district. Except for his departmental colleague with whom he had also gone to college, L had first met these men as a result of his work in Mbale. When I again interviewed him on this matter four months later, his set of friends had changed: N had been transferred and L had since become friends with P, who also worked for the co-operative and who was O's colleague. Thus, at the second interview, L's set was composed of M, O, and P, all in work related to the management or coordination of activites in the same district. The next change was recorded one month later. At this time, L named only P as his closest friend. The reduction was the result of two factors: M had been transferred and O left the organization for which he worked to join another company, in private industry, whose office was located in Kampala.

Friendship with social equals is further evident in the relationships between those of similar occupational rank (see Table 5). Elite Africans informally conceptualize three grades of occupational ranking among themselves, which they sometimes refer to as "high," "middle," and "low." These social distinctions overlap two official work grades. Those in the "high" category are senior administrators and professionals. Those in the "middle" and "low" ranks include technical and executive officers who are subdivided in terms of their income levels which are, in most cases, related to years of work experience and thus seniority. Most men select their friends from within their own occupational rank. Those in the "high" rank

Table 5. Elite Friendship Choices Within Own or Other Occupational Rank

	Own	Other	Total Choices
High (46 men)	81 (53)	40 (68)	121
Middle (37 men)	62 (35)	39 (66)	101
Low (22 men)	31 (13)	29 (47)	60
Total (105 men)	174 (101)	108 (181)	282

chose 67 percent of their friends from within that category, those in the "middle" rank chose 61 percent of their friends from their own category, and those in the "low" rank chose 52 percent of their friends from others also in the "low" rank.

The criterion of age also underlies the structure of friendship among elite Africans and is consistent with the principle of association with peers. As noted in Chapter Four, elite Africans culturally differentiate between younger and older men in terms of domestic obligations. Thus, a man, whether married or not, who has no responsibility for the care and supervision of children is considered a younger man. In contrast, a man who does assume such responsibilities is considered an older man.[2] Younger and older men are expected to, and do, spend

[2]If social age is not synonymous with chronological age there is still a relationship between them. The turning point between younger and older men is around 35 years old, varying slightly with the age at which a man first married or fathered a child. Most elite men do not marry before they are 25 years old due to the extension of their education; whereas, most non-elite men marry before they reach that age. Elite informants said that a man became "older" when the children who lived in his house and for whom he was responsible were old enough (5 to 10 years old, which may vary with the child's sex, although I did not check on this point when in the field) to "watch" the behavior of adults.

their leisure time in different ways. Younger men, for example, go out to bars almost every night, attend dances frequently and spend much time with women other than their wives. Older men pursue these activities less often and spend more time with their families. Correspondingly, most younger and older men are not together often enough to form friendships. Consistent with these differences, friendships are also made with those of similar "age": each category of men chose 85 percent of their friends from among their own age-mates (see Table 6).

The social interpretation of rank and age similarity as social equality has an interesting consequence for the friendship network of elite Africans in Mbale. If age and rank were always congruent, there would be the possibility of a division of elite friendship into at least two distinct sub-systems. In practice however, this is not the case, and the different segments are linked together in one network. High occupational rank is usually based on educational qualification. It is thus possible for young, highly educated men to be in high-ranking positions. These men have the option to associate with older men who are their occupational rank peers or with young men who are their age equals but occupationally subordinate. For example, a young doctor is able to maintain friendships with both older colleagues and younger peers. In certain situations, such as looking for women, he acts as a young man and his friends are other young elite men. In other situations, such as

Table 6. Elite Friendship Choices Within Own or Other Age Category

	Own	Other	Total Choices
Old (53 men)	111 (68)	20 (63)	131
Young (49 men)	130 (74)	24 (80)	154
Total (102 men)	241 (142)	44 (143)	285

drinking in a quiet bar, he may associate with older higher-ranking men, thereby emphasizing his professional role. Conversely, older, lower-ranked men may drink with their younger colleagues, but most often spend time with older friends with whom they have more in common, except their occupational rank. The significance of these common rank/cross age combinations is that they form a link between young and old and between the various rank categories, thereby generating a single friendship network.

Elite Africans do not consider tribal identity to be a criterion of social equality and it is not a significant factor in their friendships. Less than 10 percent of them say it is of primary importance in choosing friends, and 82 percent of their friendships are tribally heterogeneous.[3] Moreover, of those friendships which are homogeneous, individuals share other characteristics, particularly colleagueship, in addition to common ethnic identity. The Bugisu Co-operative Union is a good example of this kind of case. All the men who work in the upper echelons of the co-operative's central administration are Gisu; they also choose one another as friends. Thus, choices among colleagues in an organization which is tribally homogeneous appears to be an instance of tribal identity playing a strong role in the friendships of elite Africans.

Other data, however, support the claim that ethnicity is not a major principle in the selection of friends among elite Africans, although these materials are more difficult to interpret. For example, among central government civil servants, as in the case of the BCU, tribalism would appear at first glance to be a factor in friendship choices (see Table 7). This is partly because for historical reasons certain departments have concentrations of particular ethnic groups, and, as we have seen, choice within one's own department is high. In order to separate the influence of ethnicity from that of colleagueship, it is necessary to examine choices within one tribe and also within one department. For departments with at least two men of the same tribe, but including others from different tribes (a situa-

---

[3]Lloyd reports that over half of the friends of the new Nigerian elite in Ibadan were from ethnic groups other than their own (Lloyd 1967:146).

Table 7. Elite Friendship Choices Within Own or Other
Tribe Within Central Government

	Own	Other	Total Choices
Ganda (18 men)	16 (10)	20 (26)	36
Teso (13 men)	9 (4)	12 (17)	21
Kiga (7 men)	8 (2)	12 (18)	20
Samya (4 men)	1 (.4)	5 (5.6)	6
Soga (3 men)	1 (.4)	8 (8.6)	9
Gisu (4 men)	0 (.3)	5 (4.7)	5
Padhola (2 men)	1 (.2)	6 (6.8)	7
Gwere (3 men)	1 (.3)	5 (5.7)	6
Alcholi (6 men)	3 (.8)	7 (9.2)	10
Total (60 men)	40 (18.4)	80 (101.6)	120

tion which does not hold for the BCU), the data suggest that
tribalism is relatively insignificant (see Table 8). Thus, in situations in which both fellow tribesmen and others are available
as friends, elite Africans are just as likely to choose friends
from different tribes as they are fellow tribesmen.

To say that ethnicity is not a strong factor in elite friendships does not mean, however, that it does not influence their
behavior in other ways. Among elite Africans, tribalism is not
important structurally, that is, in the choice of friends, but it
still is important culturally in the sense that it provides certain
life-style standards. For example, one unmarried informant
when asked on what basis he would choose a wife, said:

Table 8. Elite Friendship Choices Within Own or Other Tribe Within Department Within Central Government

		Own	Other	Total Choices
Police (14 men)	Ganda (5 men)	0 (1.7)	5 (3.3)	5
	Teso (3 men)	2 (.4)	0 (1.6)	2
	Alcholi (3 men)	0 (.9)	4 (3.1)	4
Education (10 men)	Teso (4 men)	5 (4)	5 (6)	10
	Samya (2 men)	0 (.2)	1 (.8)	1
Administration (9 men)	Ganda (3 men)	2 (1.7)	3 (3.3)	5
	Kiga (3 men)	2 (1.3)	2 (2.7)	4
Agriculture (5 men)	Ganda (2 men)	1 (.4)	0 (.6)	1
	Teso (2 men)	2 (1.2)	1 (1.8)	3

I would like a girl from a reasonable family, people who have some good standard of education, who have given their children education. [Should she be of your tribe?] She should be from my own tribe, because it is the basis of some understanding. That goes for religion, too. It makes an easier marriage. But it doesn't have to be either, if we understand one another well enough.[4]

His preference for a wife is interesting, because in other respects "tribalism" is unimportant to him: his three best friends in Mbale come from three different tribal backgrounds, only

[4]More elite Africans marry women of their own tribal backgrounds (63 percent) than those of other tribal backgrounds (37 percent). Most (75 percent) of the tribally mixed marriages occur among younger elite men.

one of whom is a fellow tribesman. Moreover, he met that friend at work, not at home, unlike the pattern among non-elite Africans. His other friends include a former schoolmate and another colleague. He does not plan to retire to life in a rural area.

Just as ethnicity is not a measure of social equality, neither is common religious affiliation; 84 percent of elite friendships are religiously mixed. This fact is unusual, because in Uganda economic and political conflict is often expressed as a contrast between followers of different faiths (see Burke 1964 and Edel 1965).

Friendships among the wives of elite Africans provide an interesting comparison to those among their husbands. Their friendships parallel in certain respects those of elite men, but contrast in yet other respects where their relationships more closely resemble those among non-elite Africans, as will be seen. The wives of elite Africans value friendship, which they also believe should take place between social equals. Social equality, in their case, refers primarily to women who are also wives of elite Africans. Elite wives are itinerants, moving with their husbands from town to town. They also have met their friends before arriving in Mbale, usually through their hus-bands' work contacts. As one woman said, "You meet the wives of the men who work with your husband, and if you match, you become friends." "Matching" means primarily per-sonal compatibility. Their friendships also entail companion-ship, most often taking the form of reciprocal visiting in their homes, during which time they gossip, drink tea or beer, and do their household chores or look after their children.

The pattern of leisure-time interaction among elite wives also differs significantly from that of both elite and non-elite men. Like their husbands, elite wives choose their friends from among a pool of multi-ethnic social equals, and like non-elite men, they interact most often with nearby neighbors.

The overlap between neighbors and friends is, however, not simply a by-product of the places at which they socialize or of their domestic responsibilities. It results from the fact that few of them drive or have a car available to them during the day. Their limited physical mobility within Mbale confines their leisure-time interaction to those who live within easy walking distance, thereby producing a pattern of friendships which is dissimilar to that of their husbands, but similar to that of non-elite men.

Unlike men in either class, however, elite wives belong to voluntary associations. The most important of these are sponsored by the Y.W.C.A., the Uganda Women's Council, and the Catholic and Protestant Churches. The two church groups have religiously mixed membership, each attracting both Catholics and Protestants. In fact, the membership lists of these two clubs are practically identical; the clubs meet on different days and women attend both. The clubs meet in late afternoon, in town at the Church halls or at the Y.W.C.A. building, the women being dropped off and picked up by their husbands. The different clubs tend to schedule similar activities: instruction in English, sewing and childcare classes, and cooking demonstrations which include the use of electric kitchen appliances, the latter often conducted by employees of the Uganda Electricity Board. English classes are particularly popular since many of the wives, and particularly the older women, are less educated than their husbands and are not as socially comfortable using English, a skill which is becoming more valued and desired by them as it is increasingly expected of them by their husbands.

Regardless of their formal functions, all of the clubs provide opportunities for their members to meet and become friends with women other than their immediate neighbors. Thus, unlike their husbands, elite wives belong to corporate groups which directly express their elite status, and, unlike non-elite men, they belong to associations which bring together different neighborhood clusters, uniting different friendship sets into a single network.

Friendship among Lower-Class Africans

Lower-class Africans also choose friends in accord with a principle of association with social equals, but they use a different criterion of social equality. For them, social equality is defined primarily in terms of common tribal identity. The most significant consequence of this fact is that non-elite friendships generally do not constitute a single multi-ethnic system but, rather, a number of unarticulated networks which typically stretch between town and tribal home area.

Tribalism in the friendships of lower-class Africans in Mbale is expressed both ideologically and linguistically. They verbally emphasize the virtue of common tribal identity: 45 percent say that being of the same tribe is the most important factor in their friendships in the town. It is also evident in their use and interpretation of language. Unlike educated Africans, they do not have English as a common language. They do use Kiswahili and Luganda as trade languages, although they say that they do not like to use them in other contexts. Indeed, the language factor is most pronounced in friendship activities during which lower-class Africans use their tribal languages rather than a trade language. Moreover, when a lower-class African hears a stranger speak his own tribal language he will often introduce himself to the unknown person and assume a potential friendship on that basis alone. The comments of two informants (both Teso men) illustrate this point:

> I first met my friend in my carpentry shed. He was looking to buy furniture. When he spoke to me in Ateso [the Teso language], I gave him a good price and we became friendly.

> I first met my friend when I went to buy vegetables. When I spoke to him, he replied in a broken Luganda with a Teso accent, and so I knew him to be a Teso and we became friends.

The tribal factor is also expressed in the lower-class Africans' residence patterns in Mbale. In the rural area of the town, where there are few administrative and economic constraints on housing choices, lower-class Africans choose to live with fellow tribesmen, thereby forming distinct tribal enclaves. A typical example of this is a group of Acholi tribesmen who are friends and neighbors in a part of town commonly known for its Acholi residents. All the men live directly next to one another, having built their houses facing on a common yard to form a single compound.

The social solidarity within these tribal enclaves is recognized and used by the municipal government to maintain law
and order. In Mbale, the Municipal Agent (formerly the Township Chief) is the administrative officer who, by law and according to the Municipality's brochure, is responsible for
keeping "peace and order" among Africans residing in its rural
areas. His office is a carry-over from the period of Mbale's
history in which there were separate administrations for Africans and non-Africans (the Township District Council and the
Urban District Council, respectively). His staff is composed of
ten "chiefs" (whose duties and powers according to the town
brochure "are similar in many ways to those exercised by
chiefs in a rural district"), who represent six different tribal
groups and who are in charge of different village areas and
tribal groups. In those cases in which the Municipal Agent does
not have a link to a tribal enclave through one of his official
assistants, he works through an unofficial "headman" who
represents the group. The role of these tribal groups and their
representatives, whether official or not, reflects the significance
of tribal identity in the social organization of lower-class Africans.

This pattern of non-elite townsmen living in tribal enclaves is not limited to Mbale. The Sofers note its occurrence
in Jinja, suggesting that "tribal enclaves" there serve the function of providing a system of mutual aid to the newly arrived
members of the same tribe and that individuals in them continue to identify themselves with their fellow tribesmen rather
than with other Africans in the town (Sofer and Sofer 1955:20).
Gutkind also mentions their presence in Kampala, where they
also provide for the mutual aid of fellow tribesmen (Gutkind
1965:55).

In addition to their jural corporateness, the men in those
enclaves claim one another as best friends. Indeed, for many
lower-class Africans, especially in the rural areas of the town,
the roles of friend and neighbor are played by the same individual and they pay little attention verbally to the distinction
between these categories. Even when a non-elite African
claims as a friend a fellow tribesman who lives outside one of
these "urban villages," he still spends much of his free time

with his neighbors: 90 percent of the non-elite Africans say
that they visit socially with their neighbors, including 42 percent who say that they see their neighbors in the context of
leisure-time activities at least three times each week. The overlap between neighbor and friend is due partly to the value they
place on living next to friends and partly to the fact that they
are relatively immobile within the town, not having the means
to move safely or conveniently around at night, which limits
the spatial range of possible friendship contacts. However,
whether out of personal inclination, normative pressure, or
logistic constraint, the neighborhood is the locus of friendship
ties among lower-class Africans, and their neighborhoods tend
to be tribally homogeneous.

The partial exception to this general pattern is on the
housing estates where choice of residence is more restricted by
the limited availability of houses and where house allocation
is formally on a first come first serve basis. Since the people
living there also do not have cars and do not want to face the
danger of walking around after dark, they tend to interact with
neighbors, and where neighbors are from different tribes,
friendships tend to be tribally mixed. However, when possible,
individuals seek out as friends fellow tribesmen living in the
same housing development. Furthermore, they say that given
the choice they would rather have a fellow tribesman as a
neighbor and friend, and they try to arrange to trade houses in
order to live next to fellow tribesmen.

Thus, the cultural meanings of social equality are implied
in the structure of friendship among Africans in Mbale. Above
all other considerations, there is the division between the two
classes. Within the upper class, social equality is found among
those who are colleagues or who have common careers. Within
the lower class, social equality is found among those who are
fellow tribesmen. The connection between these friendship
choices and the emphasis on reciprocity as an ideal of friendship interaction is examined in the next chapter.

CHAPTER SIX

Managing Uncertainty

Africans in Mbale engage in friendships, and they restrict them to those individuals they think can and will meet the obligations of the relationship. The most general expectation of friendship which underlies all its particular responsibilities among both elite and non-elite Africans is reciprocity. In their view of friendship, reciprocity requires continuity of association. However, most Africans in Mbale are itinerant townsmen and their mobility potentially undermines their relationships. It does so by introducing uncertainty into social life; their mobility makes problematic the future of their relationship and thus of their potential to reciprocate. To strengthen their friendships, Africans in Mbale follow a strategy by which they attempt to reduce that uncertainty. Accordingly, they form relationships with others in which there is some degree of certainty about future interaction. That, in turn, requires the perception, implicitly or explicitly, of the circumstances and conditions which make future association probable.

The view that uncertainty about future contact is a typical characteristic of urbanism and undermines social relationships is one which appears in different approaches to the study of social order. Before examining and evaluating the strategies of Mbale's Africans for managing uncertainty, it is useful to analyze the problem in its more general form.

Urbanism and Uncertainty

Louis Wirth, in "Urbanism as a Way of Life" (1964 [1938]), suggested the thesis that uncertainty characterizes urban life and that it undermines ordered social relationships. In that essay, Wirth was concerned with variations in social "solidarity" under different conditions which he typified as "urban" and "rural." However, and as Wirth emphasized, the conditions which he labelled urban and which he associated with disorder (*Ibid.*, 82) are not limited to cities and do occur elsewhere. Also, the conditions which he labelled rural and which he associated with solidarity (*Ibid.*, 70) occur elsewhere than in the countryside, as evidenced in his own study of urban ghetto life. The conditions on which he focused, most notably population size, density, heterogeneity, and mobility, result in urbanites not knowing or having only partial and limited knowledge of one another. This anonymity sets the stage for the dissolution of social control and a corresponding increase in social disorganization (*Ibid.*, 70–72).

The link between anonymity and anomie is uncertainty. Implicit in Wirth's theory of urbanism is the view that social control is the foundation of social solidarity; and he saw uncertainty as potentially disruptive of social order because it interferes with mechanisms of social control. A system of social control involves a number of related components. First, it requires personal identity in contrast to anonymity, and a potential for future interaction or continuity of association. It also depends on the availability of sanctions and on the ability to enforce them.[1] Enforcement, in turn, requires that individuals can be located and thus subject to sanctions, and the crucial factors in locating a person are identity and continuity. Together they imply knowledge of an individual's future whereabouts, essential for the implementation of sanctions for his past and present behavior. That is, knowledge of a person which implies where he can be found "tomorrow" renders him

---

[1]Recently Pitts has suggested a similar argument in a more general discussion of social control (Pitts 1968:388).

accountable for his actions of today. Anonymity obscures such knowledge and generates uncertainty, thereby producing a breakdown in social control.

In contrast to the disorganization of urban life, rural society, in Wirth's theory, is characterized by social solidarity, based on conditions which facilitate social control. There individuals belong to corporate groups (*Ibid.*, 71–72, 81), and are known and can be located by virtue of their membership in them. Although Wirth did not examine in any detail the significance of corporate group membership, it is evident that he assumed such membership produces a degree of predictability or certainty about a person's relationships with others in almost all aspects of social life; in this sense a person is "known" and his future location can be determined. Membership in a corporate group also implies that the group or its representative is responsible for the actions of its individual members and therefore will, directly or indirectly, control their behavior.

Social control in rural life is strengthened also, as Wirth noted (*Ibid.*, 70), because in it a person's place of residence and livelihood is unlikely to change rapidly and unpredictably, further increasing his susceptability to sanctions and his conformity with the norms of his society. Furthermore, since membership in corporate groups was based directly or indirectly on kinship connections or other ties representing long-term association, there was little opportunity for an individual in the rural situation to avoid the constraints of his small-scale, local world by moving to another place in which he was not known. For reasons, then, of both corporate group structure and localized systems of social relations, Wirth ascribed to rural life social control and solidarity, and by their absence or ineffectiveness he accounted for urban social disorganization.

Although Wirth associated urbanism with disorganization, he also suggested a way by which order could be introduced into urban life. This part of his theory is consistent with his ideal-typical representation of rural society. Just as he thought that the social order of rural life is based on a system of social control exercised through kin and residential groups, he hypothesized that in urban life it should be achieved through corporate groups, although in the urban case they would be voluntary associations (*Ibid.*, 82). Again, group membership is critical in Wirth's theory. Social control and social solidarity are problematic only in the case of individuals who are "detached" from the corporate groups ("formally organized bodies") which integrate society (*Ibid.*, 76).

Although Wirth emphasized group membership, there are other structural arrangements by which individuals may be located and through which sanctions can be enforced. For example, Henslin's analysis of the "fleeting" relationship between cab-drivers and their passengers illustrates the way in which "strangers" seek to locate one another in a social network in order to gain control over the relationship.[2] Henslin describes the process of thus locating an individual in terms of "trackability" (1968:144). Henslin suggests that drivers assume greater trackability and therefore trustworthiness on the part of a potential passenger when he calls from a residentially stable neighborhood, in the belief that there is a link between the caller and others residing at his point of departure. The argument also holds for passengers: a passenger is said to be able to track a cab-driver insofar as he is identified with and traceable to a company which is easily found (and perhaps which is responsible for the actions of its employees). "Gypsy" cabs, in this respect, would be less trackable and more dangerous than cars from the fleet of an organization which has a well-known trademark.

In other contexts, as well, trackability is produced by knowledge of a person's network of family and friends. "Who do you know" (*i.e.*, where are you from, what do you do, and, by implication, who knows you) is a "game" often played by people who have just met one another and in part represents their attempt to locate themselves and others in social space. Being part of the same "small world" implies responsiveness to a relationship's norms because a person can be traced and

---

[2] J. C. Mitchell suggests that the concept of a network in social anthropological analysis is of primary importance for what it implies about a person's relations with others (his "reachability"), since social control may occur through those contacts (Mitchell 1969:5–19).

sanctioned by others (mutual friends, kin, colleagues) as well as by those directly involved in the relationship.[3] Knowledge of an individual's associates and of his place in different kinds of networks, then, is another way in which an expectation of continuity is generated, uncertainty is reduced, and social control is secured.

Social Exchange and Uncertainty

Whereas Wirth considers an expectation of future interaction in terms of its role in the process of social control, social exchange theorists focus on it in terms of its part in social interaction itself. They view a social relationship as being composed of exchange, which implies a period of time over which its give and take are transacted. Stability in a relationship requires therefore that its participants have some degree of certainty regarding not only the other's capacity and reliability for meeting the relationship's obligations, but also the probability of their future interaction necessary for the completion of the exchange.[4]

Reciprocity in particular requires a positive expectation of future interaction, as several studies suggest. Firth, for example, has noted that an expectation of "continuity of relations" is a "correlate" of reciprocity (Firth 1951:194). More recently, Sahlins has elaborated on Firth's hypothesis and developed a more complex model in which different kinds of exchange are related to different expectations of continuity of relations. For example, in "generalized reciprocity" repayment within a specific period of time is not stipulated, the implication being that the relationship is and is expected to be a long-term one (Sahlins 1965:147). As Firth also notes, the expectation of con-

---

[3]For an interesting analysis of the dimensions of a "small world," see Milgram (1967) and Travers and Milgram (1969).

[4]See, for example, Arensberg (1968:155–159), Leach (1954:153), Gouldner (1960:170, 174–175), Goffman (1970:123–130), and McCall and Simmons (1966:156, 179).

tinuity is sometimes expressed as "confidence" or "trust" in a relationship.[5] Eric Wolf makes a similar point when he writes of friendship that a display of affect, real or pretended, in a relationship may be interpreted as a mechanism for keeping it a relation of "open trust" or "open credit," a device whereby the continuity and the future of the relationship is insured (Wolf 1966:13).

Whereas trust sustains a relationship, distrust and the lack of continuity it implies undermines the solidarity of social relationships. Evidence for this correlative hypothesis is also found in Sahlin's analysis of social exchange, although in this case it comes from his example of "negative reciprocity," a short-run relationship with no expected future. It involves the attempt to get something for nothing, to take without giving, and is based on various degrees of "cunning," "guile," "stealth," and "violence." Evidence in support of the hypothesis that unpredictability or uncertainty undermines orderly social relationships also comes from Nelkin's study (1970) of life styles in migrant labor camps. She argues that disorder in the camp life of migrant laborers is related to discontinuity in the membership of working crews. Thus, in crews which are composed of a core of regular participants or which have many individuals who are related to one another as friends, hometown people, or kin, social life is not marked by tension, disputes, and interpersonal conflict. However, in crews composed of strangers, those who did not know one another before the season began and who do not expect to see one another after the season is finished, that is, of people whose relationships have no future, social life is characterized by distrust,

---

[5]Others have also noted the significance of a future orientation in the conception of confidence or trust and its importance for the maintenance of a social relationship. See Arensberg (1968:155–159), Simmel (1950:318), and Isaacs, Alexander and Haggard (1963:462). This conception of trust also extends its analysis as a property, quality, or image generated in and for a particular encounter or situation, although it is consistent with such a view since the definition of a situation also connotes through a variety of symbols a future state of events (see Goffman 1959:1–3).

animosity, and those attributes Sahlins associated with "negative reciprocity."

Thus, the management of uncertainty is, from the perspectives of both social exchange and social control theories,
critical in maintaining stability in social relationships. Managing uncertainty requires a strategy which enables an individual
to generate or confirm continuity in a relationship, the positive
expectation of future association which implies both that there
will be the time necessary for the completion of the transaction
which constitutes the relationship and that the individuals in
the relationship can be located and sanctioned and will therefore be receptive to its normative regulations. Conversely, it
requires that interaction be restricted to those with whom contact at a future time can be expected. In either case, it requires
an individual to analyze and to evaluate his and others' circumstances which will result in their recurrent interaction, that is,
to estimate the probability of their future association.

The probability of future interaction, however, cannot be
merely an outsider's analysis of the likelihood of two individuals remeeting one another. An objective view, based on statistical analysis, is not necessarily meaningful to those who
participate in a system of social relations until it is translated
into or expressed in socially relevant terms. Such "common"
knowledge entails the perception of those circumstances which
facilitate recurrent interaction, but, more importantly, it expresses them in a cultural idiom, as a sort of "social" probability, which makes them so apparent as to be thought "natural."
What these idioms are for the Africans in Mbale and the conditions which they reflect will be examined next.

Colleagueship, Tribalism and Certainty

In both the culture and structure of friendship, Africans
in Mbale act to reduce the uncertainty surrounding their relationships and thus to insure that the obligation to reciprocate
entailed in them will not be curtailed by the sudden interrup-
tions and dislocations caused by their itinerancy. Elite Afri-

cans choose friends, verbally and interactionally, from among their colleagues, and non-elite Africans similarly choose from among their fellow tribesmen. A concern for common career among upper-class Africans and for common tribe among lower-class Africans expresses the social meanings of certainty in the two classes. Moreover, colleagueship in the one case and tribalism in the other are not merely expressions of sentiment but are cultural idioms for expected future association and for the largely economic and occupational conditions which underlie the continuity in their social relationships.

The careers of elite Africans generate for them the probability and the expectation of future association, thereby sustaining their friendships. They also underlie the actual and expected discontinuities between elite and non-elite Africans. Most upper-class Africans in Uganda work for the central government, having few alternatives. The Asian population controls commerce, and the senior civil service absorbs most of the country's highly-educated and professional Africans. Not only are educated Africans limited in the fields of their employment, but once they accept a position in the civil service they tend to remain in it (see Goldthorpe 1965:64). Uganda's economy and occupational division of labor forces educated Africans into a unitary organizational system that is the basis of their social network.

The occupational structure of elite Africans underlies their recurrent interaction. During their work lives they are urban-based, stationed in Uganda's cities and towns which are its administrative and commercial centers. Moreover, they are frequently transferred around the country, and this work-based geographical mobility is conducive to the fulfillment of the reciprocity expected in friendships. Because elite Africans move from town to town, they are able to and they expect to meet over time other elite Africans and to see again those they have met before. They are aware of their continuing relationships. By giving them a sense of confidence in the continuity of their friendships, the elite Africans' itinerancy encourages them to participate in the system despite their limited stay in any one town.

Within Mbale, the boundaries of the elite Africans' social world are defined by the discontinuities in interaction between themselves and others in the town. However, their world is not a closed one. They have worked and lived in different towns throughout Uganda, they have acquaintances and friends from these experiences, and they keep in touch with them. This national network is of major significance in their adjustment to the flux of social life in urban centers like Mbale. They come to town and make contact with people they know from other places. They go to other towns with the names of their friends' friends. From the point of view of the person who remains in one place, there will be an occupational replacement who is also a potential social substitute for the friend who has been transferred. Elite Africans complain that their frequent moves are difficult since they disrupt their families' routines, especially the schooling of their children. But they do not talk about "feeling lost." This sense of integration is due to their economic independence, to their lack of a housing problem, and most significantly to the fact that socially they are not out of circulation. In what is a very fluid social situation marked by a high mobility rate, the newcomer fits into the local segment of a network of elite Africans which extends beyond Mbale.

Just as their jobs facilitate reciprocity by bringing elite Africans into contact with one another, they also enable them, and elite Africans expect to be able, to participate financially in their friendships. As employees of large-scale bureaucracies which emphasize the responsibilities and rights of seniority, elite Africans look forward to regular salary increments. Correspondingly, their incomes, if they are at the top of their salary scales, will remain high; if they are newcomers and at the beginning of their careers, their incomes will systematically be increased. Moreover, the probability and perception of regular increases in cash income further explain the rationale by which elite Africans include and exclude others from their friendships. Elite Africans who enter employment at a relatively low starting salary (those who are "low" in rank) are not automatically excluded from friendships with men who have higher incomes (those who are "high" in rank). The salary potential, if not the present income level, of these junior men legitimates their inclusion in elite social circles, since they and their friends expect them eventually to be able to reciprocate in the exchanges of friendship. For non-elite Africans, the prospects of an increasing future income are extremely slight and their economic potential for participating in the protracted reciprocity of elite friendships is practically non-existent.

Not only do the careers of upper-class Africans encapsulate them in an urban-based elite social network, but their incomes allow them to pursue a style of life which will keep them in that network and out of contact with lower-class Africans. Although elite Africans move into Uganda's urban centers because of their jobs, they are also likely to remain in or near them when they retire. Elite Africans are beginning to or are planning to build houses in Uganda's urban centers as rent-producing investments and as homes for their retirement. Others are acquiring land on the outskirts of Uganda's major urban centers—just outside a town's boundary in order to avoid municipal taxes, but close enough to enjoy the highly desirable amenities of urban life. In either case they do not plan to go back to village life. With the security from their present investments and the income they can expect from their government pensions and life insurance policies (see Table 1), they will probably not have to return.

As the elite Africans' social world is supported by occupational and economic bases, it is supported also by Uganda's educational system. Education is the main avenue to elite status, and it seems likely that, if present political and socioeconomic conditions continue, the number of elite Africans will remain small. The children of today's elite Africans will comprise the upper class of the next generation, and the division between elite and non-elite Africans will persist as a feature of Uganda's social structure. Since education, especially secondary and, increasingly, university education is basic to the formation of the African elite, the limited number of places in Uganda's schools will by itself tend to depress the size of the African elite.

The pyramid of educational opportunities in Uganda is a broad, flat one, which suggests the tremendous pressure on students seeking higher education and eventual elite status. Analysis of school enrollments indicates that in 1961 there were about 370,000 students in primary school, about 21,000 in junior secondary school, and only about 4,000 in secondary school (Hunter 1963:24; *see also* Davis 1962:357). And even with the present effort to expand primary and secondary education, it is forecast that it will be almost impossible to find places in secondary school for just 10 percent (the figure could be as low as 6 percent) of those who complete a primary education. With this constraint on the number of places in secondary school, the size of the elite will be limited, and only a select few will enter their ranks.

Furthermore, it seems very likely that those who do go on to secondary and university education will be drawn from the children of men who presently constitute the new urban elite. Primary and secondary education in Uganda is not free, and the costs of getting an education are high enough to preclude all but the relatively wealthy. In Uganda, the average per capita annual cash income is estimated at no more than $56 (Hunter 1963:8; David 1962:442). The basic costs of education per student in Uganda are approximately as follows: primary school, about $8 per year; junior secondary school, about $12 in day schools and about $98 in boarding schools per year; and secondary school, about $168 per year (Goldthorpe 1965:9; Davis 1962:346). Thus, the cost of sending just one child to junior secondary school for one year can consume almost as much as most families' annual cash income. Only the elite Africans can afford the fees for their children's secondary schooling.

There is an additional factor operating to favor the success of the children of elite Africans. In Uganda, as in other former British territories, mastery of English is essential to advancement in school and work. Hunter points out that a poor introduction to English in primary school was the major reason for failure in examinations which are essential to success not only in secondary school but which are also prerequisite to further advanced studies (Hunter 1963:5). In Uganda, until 1966 the

first years of primary school were taught in vernacular languages. Only in the much more expensive private primary
schools was English the language of instruction, frequently
taught by a native English speaker. In Mbale, there are three
such schools, and the only African students in them are children of the present upper class.[6] With this initial and more
intensive preparation, the children of elite Africans are better
equipped to compete successfully for the few places in secondary schools and in the examination at the juncture of secondary
school and university training.

In addition to economic and educational constraints, one
other factor related to the careers of elite Africans tends to
encapsulate them and to thus further their chances of continuity in their system of social relations. Most, if not all, of
the present adult generation of elite Africans were born and
raised, at least to school-age, in a rural environment. Their
early experience took place in a village context and without
major and systematic exposure to an outside world. This pattern still obtains in large part for the children of non-elite
Africans. However, the world appears to be quite different for
the children of elite Africans (*see* Lloyd 1966:27). Most of these
children are being raised in the towns in which their fathers are
working, and they are having childhood experiences which are
radically different from those of their country-located kin and
even from those of their parents. These children learn from the
strange world of television about a kind of life totally foreign
to village children; they grow up in domestic groups based to
a large extent on the nuclear family; their neighbors are not
kinsmen and this, in conjunction with the economic self-suffi-
ciency of their own families, is conducive to patterns of social

---

[6]In Mbale, elite Africans send their children to private schools whose
fees range from $13 per student per year for grades 1–6 and $35 per
student per year for grades 7 and 8 to one which charges $63 per
student per year for grades 1–8. The elite Africans spend on the
average $120 per year for school fees (see Table 1), which means that
a man would be able to send four children to primary school if he
had one child enrolled in the most expensive school ($63) and the
other three enrolled in the next most expensive schools; one in the
7th or 8th grade ($35) and two in grades 1–6 ($26).

life which are very different from those in rural areas. Moreover, their first contacts in play and in school are with children
of other elite Africans, and not only with fellow tribesmen. If
these formative years have an effect on future attitudes, it will
be one which supports the significance in their world of their
careers and which diminishes the importance of tribal loyal-
ties.

Among non-elite Africans in Mbale, tribalism provides
the foundation for and is the idiom of continuity in social
relationships. In African studies, the term "tribalism" has different meanings. Tribalism in a rural context refers to participation in a social system associated with a polity and an economy rooted in tribally controlled territory. Urban tribalism, on
the other hand, has been interpreted as a classificatory scheme,
providing categories by which African townsmen from diverse
tribal backgrounds stereotype one another to reduce the complexity of urban life. However, when townsmen must return
to their tribal homes, their tribal identity in the urban situation
seems to reflect more than a simple system of classification.
Rather, adherence to tribal customs in an urban setting is part
of the price to be paid for keeping open the opportunity to
return to the land, access to which is controlled by tribal authorities. Moreover, following tribal customs and associating
with fellow tribesmen may be seen as a statement of intention
to return home. In this sense, tribalism in urban areas represents an extension of rural tribalism, reflecting a single principle of social interaction and an interconnected set of economic
and political conditions.

Tribalism in this latter sense seems to best represent the
case of non-elite Africans in Mbale. Although they may reside
temporarily in the town, they come from and belong to the
countryside, and the prospect of their remaining rural-based is
great. There is no social security system which will provide, by
itself, for living in towns while unemployed or retired. Limited
in their income from both present and future employment, the
non-elite Africans are of economic necessity, if for no other
reasons, forced to retain links with their home areas and the
security—in the form of land for subsistence farming and the
aid and support of kin groups—found there. And, given the

persistence of present conditions, it seems likely, as Elkan suggests (1967:581–589), that despite the attractions of town life, lower-class Africans will remain tied to a system of rural-based circular migration. Thus, non-elite Africans will continue to live in a dual system, shuttling back and forth between town and tribal area. Over time, they have to return to their land and to their fellow tribesmen. This movement underlies a sense of continuity in the relationships between non-elite fellow tribesmen which maintains their ties just as the probability of renewed acquaintance in different towns supports the friendships of elite Africans.

Parkin's study of non-elite Africans in Kampala, Uganda's capital, reinforces this interpretation of the social consequences of their circular migration. The Kenyan migrants (mostly Luo and Luhya) residing on the two housing estates studied by Parkin live there for varying lengths of time but ultimately, for reasons of security, are tied to their land, homes, and kinsmen in Kenya (Parkin 1969:85, 189). Moreover, as access to land is controlled by local descent groups there is good reason for maintaining links with kin and, "by way of reinforcing these links, for adhering to customary expectations in urban domestic life" (*Ibid.*, 189). These customary expectations are primarily intra-tribal marriage (*Ibid.*, 98, 111). Thus, although his informants do not visit home as often as do non-elite Africans in Mbale, they maintain their relationships with people there by conforming to tribal custom in town, thereby expressing their loyalty and their intention of returning home. Deviation from tribal ideals of proper behavior is sanctioned by withholding friendship and by unwillingness to "recommend" a man for proper tribal marriage (*Ibid.*, 109). Intra-tribal marriage is so much taken as a sign of a man's expectation of returning home that the few cases of tribally mixed marriages which do occur happen among men and women who are of elite status and who do not "envisage" settling in their rural homes (*Ibid.*, 100).[7]

Comparison of the friendships of elite and non-elite Africans indicates that African townsmen participate in enduring

---

[7]See Chapter Five, footnote 4, page 90.

but intermittently activated systems of social relationships. Although their relationships are interrupted by geographical mobility, they are maintained by the expectation of their continuity. The idiom of the continuity for most African townsmen is that of "tribalism," a term that summarizes the conditions which support and stabilize their social relationships and which remain more or less constant over time. Among elite Africans, however, who are not subject to the same economic constraints of returning home, tribalism is relatively unimportant and is not used or thought of as a mechanism for maintaining relationships. Rather, their relationships with one another are maintained in terms of their careers which reflect the economic conditions underlying continuity in their lives. The differential emphasis on colleagueship and tribalism in upper- and lower-class friendships, respectively, reflects their efforts to restrict friendships to those with whom future interaction is most likely and thus represents their strategies for managing the uncertainty of urban social life.

CHAPTER SEVEN

Urbanism
in Other Cultures

In Mbale, the strategy for managing uncertainty and for coping with the potential disorder of urbanism calls for townsmen to confine their leisure-time interaction to those with whom future association is expected. This expectation is based on the existence and the perception of conditions, primarily economic ones, which encapsulate individuals and generate networks within which people are known and their behavior is regulated. In Mbale, the strategy is expressed in the emphasis men give to association with colleagues in the case of elite Africans, and with fellow tribesmen in the case of non-elite Africans. Consequently, within their respective networks, these townsmen do not experience the anonymity and anomie said to be typical of urbanism as a way of life. The question now is to what extent is this strategy peculiar to Africans in Uganda's urban centers. Do townsmen elsewhere face similar circumstances and employ similar strategies for coping with the complexity of urban life? This question will be examined in a comparison of urban social organization in two other cases, one in West Africa and one in the United States.

Yoruba Urbanism

The case of social organization in the Yoruba towns and cities of Nigeria in West Africa is particularly interesting because it has often been used to refute Wirth's definition of the city (see Bascom 1962, 1963). Such refutations are based on the observation that although Yoruba towns are large, dense, and permanent population centers (in the mid-50's there were ten towns with 20,000 to 50,000 inhabitants, three more towns with 50,000 to 100,000, and a further six towns with over 100,000), they do not exhibit other "urban" characteristics, in particular a sense of impersonality and anomie among their residents, thought to be features of Western industrial cities. They do not, in short, fit Wirth's conception of the city. Critics usually conclude that an understanding of urbanism would be advanced by the general acceptance of a minimal, essentially demographic, definition of a city, without reference to other sociological characteristics.

Although these discussions of terminological problems are perhaps valuable, they are misleading because they confuse, as Wirth did not, the distinction between the city on the one hand, and urbanism as a way of life on the other. Wirth argued that urbanism derived not merely from the size, density, heterogeneity, and mobility of an urban population, but from the fact that these characteristics often produce anonymity and consequently anomie. Geographical mobility in particular, and its concomitant discontinuities in social interaction, both real and anticipated, is critical in undermining urban social order. It follows from Wirth's theory of urbanism that if continuity could be maintained, then social life in a city, despite the size, density, heterogeneity, and mobility of its population could have a very different quality. It is in this sense that the example of Yoruba urban life confirms the utility of Wirth's theory and also illustrates that the strategies of Africans in Mbale are not unique to them.

The following description of Yoruba life draws on Krapf-Askari's *Yoruba Towns and Cities* (1969). That monograph documents social stability despite geographical mobility and it demonstrates that continuity in the lives of Yoruba townsmen is related to their inclusion in a system of social relations which gives them a place and an identity in society regardless of their movement into and out of various urban centers.

Yoruba towns and cities are typified by the presence of descent groups which hold and control land rights, and by the fact that citizenship in a Yoruba town is normally acquired through birth into one of these descent groups. Yoruba towns differ from most urban centers in that they include not only large populations concentrated in a nucleated residential area, but also outlying farms owned and worked by the townsmen. That is, Yoruba townsmen live within the city and commute out to work on their farms in the "suburbs," although these are legally within city limits. The Yoruba term for such an urban settlement is *ilú* and they conceptually identify townsmen as *ará ilú*, those who, by birthright, are members of an *ilú* or town (Krapf-Askari 1969:25). As with other kinship identities, this birthright ordinarily lasts a life-time, whether or not a person resides in his hometown (*Ibid.*, 26, 30–31, 33, 63, 75). This custom has two interesting implications. First, there are few "strangers" in a Yoruba town, in the sense that individuals cannot easily acquire land and settle down away from their home town, and in the sense that men are identified by particular facial scars or other diacritical marks associated with membership in particular descent groups or home towns. Secondly, since hometown identities are not affected by prolonged absences and individuals retain land rights in their home towns, rights which are difficult to acquire elsewhere, there exists a kind of tribalism similar to that found among non-elite migrants in Mbale, except that it is based on participation in a political-economic system which has urban, not rural, roots.

The organization of crafts, which constitute along with farming and trading the main occupations of most Yoruba, also lends trackability to individual townsmen. Where a craft is not controlled by kinship relationships, it is organized in "guilds" and membership in these guilds is obligatory; all practitioners of a craft within a given town must join the appropriate guild. Not only is a craftsman therefore trackable, but like Henslin's cab-drivers, he works within an organization which is well-known and which assumes responsibility for his behavior (*Ibid.*, 93–97).

Progressive Unions, associations of home-fellows banded together for the welfare and betterment of themselves and their home towns, provide another context in which Yoruba townsmen acquire identity and trackability, as well as express their expectation of returning home. These civic organizations provide a means for Yoruba townsmen to demonstrate interest in the improvement of their home towns and to show solidarity among home-fellows. Progressive Unions thus furnish Yoruba townsmen, and especially migrants away from their own towns, with a group with which they can identify and through which they symbolize their intention of returning home (*Ibid.,* 124–126; 150).

Although Yoruba townsmen, because of their membership in these different urban-based and urban-located groups, are not ordinarily "detached" and unknown individuals, there are still contexts which are typically characterized by anonymity and which produce unpredictability and uncertainty. These are situations in which individuals have no particular grounds for expecting or believing that their relationships with one another have a future; Krapf-Askari mentions market places and crossroads as examples (*Ibid.,* 113–114, 156). Significantly, the Yoruba give symbolic recognition to them. It is customary for the Yoruba to form ritual cult-groups associated with particular deities and representing collectivities of men who feel they share a common fate in important aspects of their lives. There is, however, one deity whose devotees do not gather in a group, but rather offer devotion individually and separately. He is the "god" who represents in Yoruba ritual life the absence of communal bonds and social solidarity. That is, he represents, as Krapf-Askari notes, the "principle of uncertainty" (*Ibid.,* 113).

The Yoruba townsmen who are encapsulated in these kinds of corporate groups and whose social life centers around interaction with home-fellows are for the most part small-scale farmers whose incomes are not dissimilar to those of non-elite Africans in Uganda. There is, however, a class of Yoruba townsmen who are educated and wealthy, who constitute an "elite," and who, like their counterparts in Mbale, are predominantly senior civil servants. The Yoruba elite and non-elite are also characterized by a wide gap in their incomes, and it does not derive from differences in ownership of property but from different positions within a bureaucratic occupational structure in which access to high rank is primarily by educational qualification. The similarity between the system of social stratification in Nigeria, including the Yoruba towns and cities of its western region, and Uganda is not surprising since they were both in the colonial period under British rule and are still influenced by British practices. Thus, in Nigeria's western region the annual cash income per person is about $85, the unskilled laborer gets about $210 a year, and the most skilled artisan may earn as much as $800 a year. In contrast to these men who are poorly educated are those who are highly educated (high school and college graduates), who join the senior civil service and who have incomes above $2,000 per year, along with the other perquisites (subsidized housing, loans for a car) attached to such positions. In Nigeria, like in Uganda, the compensation awarded to senior civil servants is based on standards dating from the colonial period which were created by and for British officials.

The social life of these individuals, like that among upper-class Africans in Mbale, revolves around informal interaction with other members of the elite. It varies from the Uganda pattern in that the Yoruba elite chooses its friends from among fellow elite Africans who generally are also Yoruba. Friendships among the Yoruba elite, however, are formed between individuals who often come from different towns and traditional political units (*Ibid.*, 149), a pattern which in some respects is similar to inter-ethnic friendships elsewhere. This selection from among elite Africans who are also fellow tribesmen is related in part to the fact that there is, as in some situations in Mbale, an overlap between colleagues and co-ethnics: most Yoruba civil servants are posted in either Ibadan or Lagos.

Encapsulation in corporate groups and limited opportunities to leave the "system" work to fix a Yoruba's position in a social network. Confining their interaction to others within the same or related networks reduces, for Yoruba townsmen of both elite and non-elite status, the anonymity and uncertainty potential to urban life. The probability and expectation of long-term association underwrites predictability and stability in their social relationships.

This description also holds for the non-Yoruba Africans who work and live in Yoruba towns. Cohen's analysis (1969) of Hausa traders in Ibadan, the largest Yoruba city, provides

an interesting comparison not only with their Yoruba neighbors but also with Africans in Mbale; it too demonstrates that
townsmen operate a strategy for managing uncertainty that is
based on conditions which encourage their long-run association and cooperation.

In the case of the Hausa, the management of uncertainty
is extremely profitable, since it underlies the trade of cattle and
kola nuts which stretches between south-western and northern Nigeria. This trade is based on credit which is given and
received between men who are often "total strangers" to one
another (*Ibid.,* 6, 16, 37–39). The trustworthiness of the local,
Ibadan-based Hausa "landlords" who mediate between the
dealers from the North and from the South is therefore critical
to the stability of the credit system which is based on informal,
moral and ritual sanctions rather than on political and legal
mechanisms (*Ibid.,* 5, 84–86).

The mediators of the Hausa Quarter in Ibadan, who play
such crucial roles in the organization of long-distance trade are
its most "settled" men, a fact which underwrites their trustworthiness. Analyses of the ways in which men become settled
in the Quarter and the meaning of being settled there are basic
to an understanding of the Hausa credit system. To begin with,
the Hausa Quarter (*Sabon Gari* or *Sabo*) in Ibadan, like its
counterparts in other Yoruba towns, is headed by a Hausa
chief who is recognized as such by the local authorities and
who is responsible for the conduct of his people (*Ibid.,* 9, 21).
The Hausa of *Sabo* distinguish between a settler and a stranger,
a distinction which does not wholly rest on the criterion of
length of residence but rather indicates differing degrees of an
individual's investment in the Quarter and of his trackability
which is associated with that investment.

There are five criteria of settlement. The most important
is rights in permanent housing. Without an investment in
housing in the Quarter a man will have no "creditworthiness"
within it, and its most trusted residents are the thirty business
landlords who control more than half of the housing of the
Quarter. The Quarter Chief controls, by his granting or withholding approval, the sale of houses or rights in housing. A
man, therefore, cannot easily pull out of the Quarter in order
to escape from his financial obligations (*Ibid.,* 34, 71–72).

A second standard of settlement and thus of trustworthiness is that of occupational role. Most trusted are those whose roles represent the highest degree of commitment to permanent settlement in the Quarter and which involve the greatest investment, in both financial and personal terms, in the local community. Such investment is marked in the amounts of money invested in giving credit, loans, or presents which are required by the occupation, of income which the role yields, and of experience and training in local conditions which the role necessitates (*Ibid.*, 34–5). This last point is especially important since it includes the "connections" an individual has with people in the Quarter, in Ibadan, in the North, and in other Hausa communities in the South—all of which further identify a man and implicate him in a network which renders him traceable and subject to controls.

The other criteria are the residence of a man's family, his primary relationships within the Quarter, and his relationship with the Chief. The whereabouts of a man's wife or wives and children is not very significant since divorce and child-fostering is easy and common among Hausa Moslems. A wife's residence increases in importance if she was born in Ibadan and if her parents live in the Quarter; these factors imply points of attachment to the community and nearby sources of support and sanctions. Primary relationships, particularly friendships within the Quarter are indicators of a man's settlement insofar as they involve the "total personalities" of the friends (*Ibid.*, 36–37). Those presumably afford extensive knowledge about an individual on the basis of which his future behavior can be predicted. Finally, a man is considered settled and trustworthy to the extent that he identifies himself with and pays allegiance to the Quarter Chief. This is another example of "who do you know-who knows you?", since not only is the Chief responsible for his people's behavior but, as Cohen notes, the Chief is an indispensable reference for a man's honesty and creditworthiness.

Cohen's analysis of the Quarter "landlords" demonstrates that their social and economic credit worthiness reflects an expectation of continuity in their relationships. They are permanent settlers whose trackability contrasts sharply with that of the migrants and strangers who temporarily lodge in the

Quarter. In the flux and flow which characterizes African urban life, they maintain a framework which ensures structural
stability despite the mobility of various segments of the population (*Ibid.*, 71, 96, 119). In the networks of Hausa social and
economic relationships which stretch between urban centers,
they act as "social landmarks," as pillars of the community,
helping to maintain the social organization of Hausa traders in
Yoruba towns.

Urbanism in the United States

In African urban centers, townsmen live in separate social
worlds within which they have and are confident of continuing
relationships. Within their social networks, whether class or
tribal, they are able to reduce the problems of dealing with
strangers and other outsiders and they are able to maintain
orderly social relationships. In urban America, too, individuals
withdraw to the safety of networks composed of people they
know and trust—kin, friends, colleagues, neighbors.

This strategy is evident from a number of recent field
studies. One example is Gerald Suttles' *The Social Order of the
Slum* (1968). Suttles' study of an ethnically and racially heterogeneous "slum" area in Chicago's Near West Side demonstrates that social solidarity is built on a sense of continuity in
social relationships and that people maneuver to confine their
relationships to those with whom continuous interaction can
be established or confirmed. Slum residents, Suttles argues,
face uncertainty not only because they live within a particularly transient world but because they appear, as slum residents, to be untrustworthy. By the standards of middle-class
society, Suttles writes, they do not inspire the levels of trust
necessary for communal life (*Ibid.*, 6). That is, although individual slum residents may not believe that they themselves
are as dangerous as middle-class opinion holds them to be,
what they do not know, and therefore what undermines their
social relationships, is whether or not their neighbors are trustworthy (*Ibid.*, 26).

To deal with this uncertainty, slum residents employ, according to Suttles, a combination of strategies. The most important of these, from the point of view of establishing secure relationships, are to take refuge within the family, to retreat to a circle of co-ethnics, and to establish "personal" relationships (*Ibid.*, 26). These strategies all connote a sense of continuity. Withdrawing to the household means falling back on kinsmen and the continuity implied in that relationship.[1] Ethnic encapsulation similarly implies continuity, since co-ethnics are neighbors and the constraints of long-term co-residence invest ethnicity with kin-like qualities. This is particularly the case for the Italians in Suttles' area. The distinction between the bonds among residentially immobile neighbors and those among co-ethnics is especially important, because ethnicity itself is not enough to guarantee social solidarity. Rather, it appears to be the idiom—much as tribalism is in Africa—of long-term association, experienced in the past and expected in the future (*Ibid.*, 28, 34–35, 98–107). Establishing a personal relationship does not necessitate sharing kinship, ethnicity, or locality, but does require that individuals reveal a great deal of information about each other's character and personal history, including the kinds of details which provide a basis for prediction about future behavior.

Consistent with his theory about the basis of social order, Suttles argues that residential mobility promotes social instability and disorder (*Ibid.*, 8, 124, 181, 188). He bases his conclusion on a comparison of the Italians, Mexicans, Puerto Ricans, and blacks who live in the slum area. These four "ethnic sections" occupy different points on a continuum of geographical

---

[1]See Schneider's argument that in American culture kinship is conceptualized as a permanent relationship (Schneider 1968:123–29, 91). A similar argument is presented in a recent monograph on English kinship patterns, the companion study to Schneider's analysis. Firth and his colleagues write of kinship relations among middle-class Londoners that there is "the recognition of the kinship bond as one marked by continuity" (Firth 1970:387). Fortes, making cross-cultural comparisons, has analyzed the implication of expected continuity in kinship relations. See his *Kinship and the Social Order* (Fortes 1969), especially chapters 12 and 13.

mobility with Italians being the most stable residentially and blacks the least stable. This variation in mobility correlates with stability of social relations; the Italians are characterized by greater stability and solidarity, while the transient blacks are described as being estranged from one another and their interaction is said to be characterized by anonymity and distrust (*Ibid.*, 9, 124).

In reaching this conclusion, Suttles is confirming a commonly held opinion that geographical mobility undermines social solidarity.[2] But, as we have seen in the examples of African townsmen, this is not necessarily the case. Itinerant townsmen can and do participate in a system of social relations marked by continuous, if intermittent, interaction. They experience stability and solidarity, but find it among people who travel the same routes, not necessarily among those who occupy a particular locality. It is possible that in Chicago's Near West Side the significant contacts of the transient blacks are not found in that neighborhood, that it is not for them, as it is for the long-resident Italians, the center of their social world. It is also possible that the geographically mobile blacks are encapsulated within non-localized networks and that they are less disorganized than Suttles suggests. Unfortunately, there is not enough evidence in Suttles' description of the blacks to evaluate the extent of their social disorganization.

There are some data in Eliot Liebow's *Tally's Corner* (1967), a study of transient streetcorner men in Washington, D.C., but Liebow does not develop its significance for this question. In fact, Liebow interprets the relationships of streetcorner men in accord with the theory that transiency produces social instability. He argues that the instability of their friendships is related to their uncertainty about their future association, a conclusion which is theoretically consistent with the hypothesis that social solidarity is based on an expectation of future interaction. However, the facts of Liebow's case do not fully support his interpretation, and this apparent discrepancy invites a reconsideration of that part of his argument.

---

[2]See, for example, Gans 1967:311, Cloward and Ohlin 1960:172, and Keller 1968:61.

The subjects of *Tally's Corner* are geographically mobile men who for various reasons move into and out of the locality which Liebow studied. Their transiency, Liebow suggests, undermines the stability of their social relationships. Although what constitutes social instability is not explicitly defined in *Tally's Corner,* implicitly it means short-lived interaction (*Ibid.,* 70–78, 162–163, 204–207). Using this conceptualization, it is difficult, given the frequent moves of the streetcorner men into and out of the neighborhood, to consider their relationships anything but unstable. However, a different interpretation could be placed on their relationships if they were viewed not in terms of a single place and moment in time, but over a longer period and within wider boundaries defined interactionally. That is, using another framework of analysis, their relationships might be regarded as enduring but only intermittently activated.

Liebow's ethnography seems to support this alternative view, although again there is not enough information to satisfactorily confirm or reject either interpretation. There is, for example, the case (*Ibid.,* 192ff.) of two men who first met one another away from the place Liebow studied and earlier than the time of his field work, and who had been close friends until they moved to different neighborhoods. Two years after this interruption, they re-met and re-established their friendship for several months before once again moving apart. Such continuity is not limited to friendships; kin and affines see each other again and again, even though they are dispersed between the rural South and the urban Northeast. Although it is possible to assume that these men infer, from their past and present contacts, that they will see one another again, there is no direct information on whether or not they expect to re-meet at a future time.

Although there is insufficient data in *Tally's Corner* to "test" the relationship between anticipated interaction and social stability, there is more evidence in at least two other works: Claude Brown's *Manchild in the Promised Land* (1965) and Ulf Hannerz' *Soulside* (1969). Brown's account of ghetto life describes young men growing up in Harlem who are continuously moving from one city to another, and from street life to

prison life. Necessarily, they often lose contact with one another. Yet, their friendships persist for years, being renewed as
they cross paths both in and out of jail (*Ibid.*, 251–257, 375–
380). Even when they do not meet face-to-face, they keep
track of one another in streetcorner gossip (*Ibid.*, 202, 212, 304,
380, 418–425). Moreover, Brown and his friends anticipated
seeing one another off and on over the long-run; they expected
to meet and re-meet because their prospects were those of
moving between street life and prison, a pattern of "circular
migration" underlying the persistence of their relationships.

A similar account is contained in *Soulside.* Hannerz' study
is particularly interesting since it is based on observations
made among ghetto residents in Washington, D.C., the site of
Liebow's field work. Hannerz describes a category of men who
resemble those dealt with by Liebow; regularly unemployed
men who are sometimes in the neighborhood and sometimes
out of it. Although these men are transients, their social relationships are not unstable; they keep up with friends and kinsmen who are not in their neighborhood. He also describes
"Southern migrants" who keep in touch with the people back
home by visiting during holidays or by sending children to
spend part of summer vacation with their cousins; "Main-
streamers" who live in one place, but who have most of their
friends scattered over town and in other cities, and with whom
they maintain contact by visiting; and "swingers" who are
highly mobile residentially and who participate in widely dispersed networks, the links of which are renewed at various
social occasions (dances, picnics) and through gossip between
mutual friends (Hannerz 1969:24–27, 40–45).

Although these studies do not provide conclusive evidence that relatively uneducated and poor transients in American cities are encapsulated within networks supported by a
pattern of "circular migration" analogous to that among most
African townsmen, the hypothesis is not an unreasonable one.
Being unskilled, these men have little job security, and they are
forced by their circumstances to move frequently in search of
employment and a place to live. With little income, they gravi-
tate towards low-rent districts. Occupational, economic, and
other socio-political constraints tend to limit them to move-

ment between ghettoes, or between urban and rural pockets of poverty. Meeting and re-meeting the same people in different places seems a likely pattern.

The same pattern, among a different category of workers, is evident in William Whyte's *The Organization Man* (1956), his study of middle-class "transients" whose situation and system of social relations bear a close resemblance to those of elite Africans in Mbale. They also are employees of large-scale public and private bureaucracies, are transferred from city to city, and have their social relationships interrupted by these frequent re-locations. They also are encapsulated within a social network based on their common careers, within which they enjoy a sense of belonging and social solidarity. In fact, Whyte describes them as being rootless in the old geographical and fixed sense of that term, but suggests that through their common styles of life and patterns of mobility, they find a new basis for stability in their social relationships (*Ibid.*, 319–320, 329). Moreover, this stability is based on expected continuity. As organization men, their careers offer them the likelihood of continuing social relationships despite their geographical mobility. As they move from one place to another they are almost bound to meet fellow transients, with a good chance that some of them will be people that they have met before. The chances are also good of running into one another in still another place. These itinerants conceptualized this probability and their expectation of continuity in their social relationships by believing that they live in a "small world" (*Ibid.*, 305–306).

Thus, the strategy of townsmen in Uganda for constructing social order is similar to that found among urbanites elsewhere. In the urban centers of both West Africa and the United States, individuals form themselves into separate small worlds. For those who are residentially stable, the small worlds are local communities; for those who are migrants or itinerants, the small worlds are social networks. Within both the local community and the social network, individuals anticipate and realize recurrent interaction, thereby reducing anonymity and uncertainty. Within the local community and social network, individuals experience a sense of identity and a measure of solidarity.

CHAPTER EIGHT

Conclusion

Africans in Mbale, as well as in Uganda's other urban centers, are itinerant townsmen. Elite Africans move from town to town and non-elite Africans circulate between town and tribal home; the geographical mobility of both classes is conditioned by economic constraints and occupational opportunities. This mobility is potentially disruptive of social order because it introduces an element of uncertainty into social relationships, and uncertainty undermines ordered social interaction because it impedes both the exchange which constitutes a relationship and the enforcement of sanctions which control a relationship. Africans in Mbale cope with this uncertainty by confining their relationships, when possible, to those individuals with whom they expect to be in contact at a future time, a strategy which requires their perception of the conditions which will result in recurrent interaction. For elite Africans, that expectation and the conditions on which it is based are expressed in their friendship with colleagues; for non-elite Africans, they are manifest in the social solidarity among fellow tribesmen.

Expected continuity of association by itself is not sufficient to insure the stability of a relationship, although its absence seems enough to undermine it. Africans in Mbale choose their friends on the basis of common interests, a standard which connotes to them personal compatibility. Friends are men who, for whatever psychological reasons, find one another

good company. Sociologically, however, common interests reflect social equality, and Africans in Mbale interpret that in
terms of their experience and expectation of long-term, continuous, although perhaps intermittent, interaction.

The history and anticipation of association are equally
significant, and although often related, they do not necessarily
imply one another. For example, a man interacts with a friend
at some time in the past, discontinues seeing him, and then
renews the relationship. From his present-time perspective, he
is able to infer that if conditions remain relatively constant, he
will probably interact with that friend at a future time even if
their relationship is again temporarily interrupted. But it is also
possible for two individuals to expect future association on the
basis of present position and constant conditions, even if
previously they had not known one another; they extrapolate
from the present to the future without reference to the past.
Thus, elite Africans of different tribal backgrounds become
friends, knowing that on the basis of their elite status and the
conditions which it reflects they are of the same "small world"
and are therefore social equals.

It is possible to analyze the consequences of the geographical mobility of Mbale's Africans and the conditions which
foster it from different perspectives. The main focus in this
study has been its effect on the stability of social relationships
and on network integration. Elite Africans choose friends from
among colleagues, and tribalism is not an important factor in
their choices. The evidence for the insignificance of tribal identity is that most of their friendships are tribally mixed and that
tribalism does not play an important role in their beliefs about
social stratification and in their culture of friendship.

There is, moreover, some other evidence to support the
contention that the status, life style, and culture of elite Africans sets them apart from their non-elite fellow tribesmen.
Additional data come from a political event, a context of interaction in which elite Africans were able to choose among
alternative courses of action. The particular example involves
the political crisis in Uganda in May, 1966, when the central
government's forces fought with Ganda tribesmen who were
defending the government of the traditional ruler (the Kabaka)

of Buganda, a largely autonomous kingdom within the then federation of political units which comprised the state of Uganda. The contexts of friendship and politics are critical because in them choices are possible and when they are made allegiances are revealed.

Writing just prior to Ugandan independence, L.A. Fallers suggested that one key to the development of nationalism in Uganda would be the emergence of a culture which would unite its ethnically diverse population (Fallers 1961:677). He also predicted that in Uganda this process could be complicated by the independent identity of the Ganda, the country's largest tribe, noting that the Ganda would have to either secede from the national federation or accept an extra-tribal system of values and beliefs (*Ibid.,* 685). Thus, the reaction of Ganda elite Africans in Mbale at the time of a revolution that forcibly incorporated the Ganda kingdom into the country's present unitary administrative structure provides a crucial test of their place in and commitment to a multi-tribal elite social network.

The Ganda elite Africans working and living in Mbale are typical in their friendship patterns of the elite as a whole. Their friendships are ethnically and religiously heterogeneous and are wholly contained within the elite. Of 31 elite Ganda friendship sets, only one is ethnically homogeneous and only one is religiously homogeneous. In their choices of friends in Mbale, Ganda elite Africans do not confine themselves to their fellow tribesmen.

The reaction of Ganda elite Africans in Mbale to the central government's overthrow of the government of Buganda is consistent with their acceptance of a multi-tribal, Uganda-wide social network and of the culture of friendship, including the unimportance of tribal identity as a criterion of social equality, which lies behind it. In May, 1966, central government forces acted to support a newly-introduced constitution which severely curtailed the traditional authority of the Kabaka of Buganda. The Kabaka is the primary political and cultural symbol of the Ganda (Richards 1964:286–288). Great numbers of Ganda tribesmen living in the rural areas of Buganda rose in revolt, in support of their ruler and against the central government. In a series of bloody battles, many of these

Ganda were killed, the Kabaka's palace was destroyed, and the Kabaka was forced to flee the country. The allegiance of most Ganda to the Kabaka and to Ganda separatism was overwhelmingly demonstrated in their resistance to the central government.

In contrast to the action of the mass of Ganda tribesmen, the elite Ganda in Mbale did nothing to support the government of Buganda or to defend the person of the Kabaka. Their response is especially significant because, as Richards notes, traditionally a Ganda "was expected to give his life for a king or a prince, not only in battle, but on all occasions when the royal person was threatened" (*Ibid.*, 277–278). At the time of the revolution, there were 15 Ganda upper-class Africans present in the town and the reaction of these men suggests that their allegiance to the Kabaka is subordinate to their other, non-tribal, interests. None of them left town to go to Buganda to defend the Kabaka. When asked if they were planning to go, some answered that their first responsibility was the safety and well-being of their families (their wives and children) who were with them in Mbale. Others said that they were civil servants and could not afford to jeopardize their jobs.

What factors might account for the appearance in these men of beliefs and values which support an extra-tribal political order? Are Ganda who have non-Ganda friends and who did not rally to the Kabaka in some way marginal to Ganda society and for that reason less committed to a separate Ganda political entity? Whatever other factors that explain their behavior, data about the personal attributes of these men suggest that they are not generally divested of an interest in Ganda society. All but one could claim land in Buganda. Most of the married men have Ganda wives. Nor are these men primarily from traditionally non-elite families as indicated by their father's occupations; half were cultivators but the others were chiefs or skilled workers. Finally, even if it were assumed that younger men would be less committed to the Ganda political establishment, their extra-tribal values can not be explained by reference to their ages; they are divided almost evenly between those under 30, those between 30 and 40, and those over 40. The reason for their extra-tribal values seems to be found not in their lack of interest in Ganda society, but rather in their incorporation in a non-tribal social network which, in turn, is based on a national economic-occupational system.

The focus of this study is not only on integration within the elite Africans' network, but also on their separation from non-elite fellow tribesmen. This division indicates the social distance between them, and it also underlines the importance of the geographical mobility of Mbale's elite Africans. The significance of their movement is evident when the itinerant elite Africans in Mbale are compared with the less mobile Yoruba elite. Although the Yoruba choose their friends from among socially equal colleagues and others of elite status, their solidarity with less fortunate kinsmen continues (Krapf-Askari 1969:140–141), unlike the pattern among elite Africans in Mbale. This solidarity is consistent with the fact that elite Yoruba are usually posted in Ibadan and are likely, and expect, to spend their entire careers in that one place, without being transferred from one town to another (Lloyd 1967:131; Krapf-Askari 1969:146). The Yoruba elite in comparison to Uganda's elite Africans, are not itinerant townsmen, and the maintenance of bonds between elite and non-elite Yoruba correlates with the high probability of their future association.

This contrast to the pattern in Uganda appears to be related also to other differences in the economic and political conditions in the two cases, which effect the likelihood of continuing association between elite and non-elite kinsmen. Unlike in Uganda's urban centers, most land in and around Yoruba towns and cities is still vested in corporate descent groups (Krapf-Askari 1969:135). Thus, when an elite Yoruba returns from Ibadan to his home town, which he is constrained to do since land in other Yoruba urban centers is controlled by kin groups other than his own, he returns to his non-elite kinsmen who control access to the land on which he settles. They cannot, in contrast to elite Africans in Mbale, easily avoid recurrent interaction with and dependence on their non-elite kinsmen.

The social consequences of geographical mobility are evident also among non-elite Africans who have different patterns of movement. In Mbale, non-elite Africans circulate between the town and their tribal homes. They expect to have on-going relationships with their kinsmen and fellow tribesmen as a correlate of their pattern of migration and the economic conditions under which it persists. However, there are non-elite Africans elsewhere in Uganda who are itinerant townsmen, and who move not between town and country, but between urban centers. Parkin's study of Kenyans in Kampala focuses on Luo and Luhya tribesmen who must return to their tribal land and who therefore maintain social solidarity with their kin and fellow tribesmen both in the city and in the country. However, Parkin notes, there are non-elite Luo and Luhya in Kampala who do neither (Parkin 1969:178 n.2; *see also* Grillo 1969:299, 320). These men work for the East African Railways and Harbors, an organization which transfers its workers, elite and non-elite, from town to town throughout East Africa. They are encapsulated in their own urban-based social network which is supported by a unitary organizational framework. They are not subject to the same constraints as other non-elite townsmen, they do not participate in tribal associations as do the non-railway workers in Kampala, nor are their relationships with one another particularly influenced by the standard of tribal identity.

The difference in the behavior of non-elite townsmen who expect to return to their tribal homes and those who do not is illustrated also in Mayer's study (1961) of South African migrant laborers. When Xhosa tribesmen go to work in East London, South Africa, they maintain their relationships with those who remain in the rural areas by returning home periodically and by associating with home-fellows while in town. It is, however, not only the practice of returning home which renews and sustains their relationships, thereby keeping the migrants encapsulated in their networks, but also their expectation of doing so. This comes out clearly in Mayer's discussion of the differences between those who maintain their relationships, the "home-visitors," and those who let them lapse, the "absconders" (Mayer 1961:95, 96). The home-visitor's behavior with his home-fellows in town is regulated by his anticipation of returning home and the future sanctions on his present behavior (*Ibid.*, 104). On the other hand, for the absconders who do not expect to return home, threats of future sanctions by the people at home are meaningless (*Ibid.*, 132–133). Thus, for migrant laborers in South Africa, as in Uganda, the anticipation of future behavior shapes their relationships with fellow tribesmen in the urban context.

In addition to the analysis of its effects on network integration, the individual's view of his itinerancy is another perspective on the consequences of geographical mobility. Many elite informants in Mbale talk about the disruptions to family life caused by their frequent and sudden transfers. Interruption of their children's schooling is the problem they mention most often. Some informants describe the difficulties in establishing social clubs or other group activities in Mbale that result from the rapid and unpredictable turnover of elite Africans. Others recognize that their own social lives and friendships do not suffer too much from their movement; they understand that as some friends leave others will arrive and that there is a good chance of renewing contact with a friend who is transferred away. However, none of the Africans in Mbale talk about the system-wide consequences of their movement. That perspective, in this case, is mine.

Other analysts have a different view of the consequences of geographical mobility. Wirth, for example, saw it as disruptive in the cases of free-floating individuals, those who were "detached" from organized groups. The distinction Wirth made between its effects on isolated individuals and on other urbanites is often overlooked in urban studies by those who see geographical mobility as essentially disruptive. The reasons for this oversight are not clear, although there are several possible factors. Wirth perceived encapsulation and the reduction of urban anonymity and anomie primarily in terms of an individual's attachment to or membership in corporate groups, which, in his theory, were essential for social order. In part, this reflected Wirth's attempt to identify in the urban context social units which were structurally similar and functionally analogous to those which he believed were the bases of social solidarity in the rural society. Many urbanites, however, do not belong to or participate in voluntary associations; and for those who do, membership does not seem to be critical to the organization of their extra-associational social relationships. Thus, Wirth's emphasis on corporate group membership as the primary mode of encapsulation may have misled some researchers into discounting his differentiation of mobility among different types of urbanites and of its different social consequences.

The other reasons appear to derive from certain methodological inadequacies in urban research. Many studies of urban social organization have been "community" studies, in which it has been assumed that the boundaries of a "community" are congruous with a specific locality. Social scientists working within this framework tend to study places—neighborhoods, cities—rather than systems of social relationships. Concepts and methods of research appropriate for the study of locality, however, often preclude the adequate interpretation of the social relations of geographically mobile individuals. This type of problem has led to the development of network analysis.

Although network analysis has proved useful in describing the structure of social interaction among itinerant townsmen and others whose relationships are not contained within corporate groups, it raises other problems. One of the most important of these involves the question of what Mitchell has referred to as the "durability" of a network (Mitchell 1969:26). A network is composed of social relationships between pairs of individuals. Some of the relationships in which an individual is involved may be mobilized at one time, but others are not and remain "latent" until they are activated. The problem is what accounts for the maintenance or durability of a network during periods of latency in the relationships which define it. In the present study, this problem takes the form of what sustains a relationship when it is disrupted by geographical mobility or, in other terms, under what conditions are social relationships stable when they are only intermittently activated, as in the case of itinerant townsmen.

The general answer to this question as suggested by the cases examined in this study, is that social relationships are stable when the individuals involved in them can expect future association with one another. The basis for such an expectation may be primarily economic (colleagueship, tribalism), but it also may be ideological. Many ideologies of kinship, for example, imply life-long relationships regardless of the frequency of their activation (see Schneider 1968, Fortes 1969, and Firth, Hubert, and Forge 1970). Of course, kinship ideology may be a cultural idiom for economic factors, although the precise relationship between them is still a debatable issue. Whatever its particular bases or idioms, it is useful to state in general terms the relationship between an expectation of continuity and the stability of a social relationship; the general form facilitates comparative analysis and, for the ethnographic materials reviewed in this book, it encompasses different cultural idioms and pragmatic constraints and it applies both to those who are geographically mobile and to those who are residentially stable.

It is important, however, to work also with the different cultural idioms and the belief systems of which they are a part. A people's values, beliefs and norms not only provide an outsider with guidelines for the observation of their patterns of interaction, but also a standard for the analysis of their behavior. Elite Africans, for example, speak of themselves collectively as "we," in contrast to non-elite Africans, and they use "upper class" and "lower class" as terms of reference. These terms are the elite Africans' abstractions of or shorthand for complex social and cultural facts, just as I use the concept of a "network" to analyze and describe the "same" set of facts. These folk categories were among the first data I collected in the field. In many ways they are the "easiest" to obtain, and without them it would have taken much longer and perhaps it would not have been possible to get at the social reality to which they refer.

That does not mean that I could simply accept what informants said about what they do, but that their statements suggested to me directly and indirectly important areas for detailed research. Hence, the elite Africans' use of "upper class" and their explanation of its meaning led me to ask questions about individuals' education, occupation, and income, as well as about who drank with whom, where, and in which social contexts. Their ideas also made intelligible why people with similar incomes, for example, the up-and-coming young elite Africans and the old established non-elite Africans who had no further prospects, were not always included within the same social category. Similarly, their ideas about social equality, reciprocity, and respectability made sense of their differential evaluation of "similar" leisure-time activities among elite and non-elite men, as well as among "younger" and "older" elite men, and of the social division between elite and non-elite Africans. Thus, the data I collected, which constitute the basis of my analysis, include both belief systems and patterns of action.

Insofar as people's ideas and behavior and the relationship between them are the focus of analysis, urban anthropology does not differ methodologically from field work done in other places. This focus of analysis and description is well demonstrated in anthropological urban studies (see, for example, Fortes 1949 and Mitchell 1961), although sometimes it is overlooked as anthropologists turn to urban research in their own society, as well as in other cultures.

There is also a similarity of problem orientation between this study of itinerant townsmen and other non-urban ethnographies. For example, Evans-Pritchard's classic study (1940) of the transhumant Nuer of the southern Sudan is concerned with the question of social order among a geographically mobile population, and Turner's analysis (1957) of schism and continuity among the Ndembu of Zambia also focuses on the ways in which individuals cope with the problems associated with residential instability. Moreover, both these studies indicate that the expectation of recurrent interaction underlies the stability of social relationships.

That these rural societies are also characterized by population mobility suggests that it is useful to reconsider the nature of "urbanism as a way of life" and the "fleeting" relationships of which it is composed. There is little doubt that urbanites enter into relationships which end quickly. But there are also others which, although activated only intermittently, continue over long periods of time. From the point of view of the time and place at which they are activated, they may appear as transient as other short-run terminal interactions. Yet, they differ precisely because they do persist, and the study of itinerant townsmen in Uganda illustrates that difference.

Bibliography

Arensberg, Conrad
  1968 *The Irish Countryman* (originally published 1937). New York: The National History Press.

Bascom, William
  1962 "Some Aspects of Yoruba Urbanism," *American Anthropologist* 64:4:699–709.
  1963 "The Urban African and his World," *Cahiers D'Etudes Africaines* 4:14:163–185.

Bohannan, Laura
  1952 "A Genealogical Charter," *Africa,* 22, 4.

Brown, Claude
  1965 *Manchild in the Promised Land.* New York: Signet.

Burke, Fred G.
  1964 *Local Government and Politics in Uganda.* Syracuse: Syracuse University Press.

Cloward, R. A. and L. E. Ohlin
  1960 *Delinquency and Opportunity: A Theory of Delinquent Gangs.* Glencoe: The Free Press.

Cohen, Abner
  1969 *Custom and Politics in Urban Africa.* Berkeley and Los Angeles: University of California Press.

Coleman, J. S.
  1958 "Relational Analysis: the Study of Social Organization with Survey Methods," *Human Organization* 17:28–36.

Davis, H. David (ed.)
    1962 *The Economic Development of Uganda.* Baltimore: The
        Johns Hopkins Press.

Denzin, Norman K.
    1970 "Rules of Conduct and the Study of Deviant Behavior:
        Some Notes on the Social Relationship," in *Social
        Relations* (ed. George J. McCall) pp. 62–94. Chicago:
        Aldine Publishing Company.

Edel, May
    1965 "African Tribalism: Some Reflections on Uganda,"
        Political Science Quarterly LXXX:357–372.

Elkan, Walter
    1967 "Circular migration and the growth of towns in East
        Africa," *International Labor Review* 96:581–589.

Epstein, A. L.
    1964 "Urban Communities in Africa," in *Closed Systems and
        Open Minds* (ed. M. Gluckman) pp. 83–102. Chicago:
        Aldine Publishing Company.

Evans-Pritchard, E. E.
    1940 *The Nuer.* London: Oxford University Press.

Falloro, Lloyd A.
    1961 "Ideology and Culture in Uganda Nationalism,"
        American Anthropologist 63:4:677–686.
    1964 "The modernization of social stratification," in *The
        King's Men* (ed. L. A. Fallers) pp. 117–157. London:
        Oxford University Press.

Fararo, T. J. and M. H. Sunshine
    1964 *A Study of a Biased Friendship Net.* Syracuse: Syracuse
        University Press.

Firth, Raymond
    1951 *Elements of Social Organization.* Boston: Beacon Press.

Firth, R., H. Hubert and A. Forge
    1970 *Families and Their Relatives.* London: Routledge and
        Kegan Paul.

Fortes, M.

1949 "Time and Social Structure," in *Social Structure* (ed. M.
Fortes) pp. 54–85. New York: Russell and Russell, Inc.

1969 *Kinship and the Social Order.* Chicago: Aldine Publishing
Company.

Gans, Herbert S.

1967 "Urbanism and suburbanism as ways of life: a
re-evaluation of definitions," in *The Study of Society* (ed.
P. I. Rose) pp. 306–322. New York: Random House.

Goffman, Erving

1959 *The Presentation of Self in Everyday Life.* New York:
Doubleday and Company, Inc.

1970 *Strategic Interaction.* Philadelphia: University of
Pennsylvania Press.

Goldthorpe, J. E.

1965 *An African Elite.* Nairobi: Oxford University Press.

Gouldner, Alvin W.

1960 "The norm of reciprocity: a preliminary statement,"
American Sociological Review 25:161–178.

Grillo, R. D.

1969 "The Tribal Factor in an East African Trade Union," in
Tradition and Transition in East Africa (ed. P. H.
Gulliver) pp. 297–322. Berkeley and Los Angeles:
University of California Press.

Gutkind, P. C. W.

1965 "African Urbanism, Mobility and the Social Network,"
in *Kinship and Geographical Mobility* (ed. R. Piddington)
pp. 48–60. Leiden: E. J. Brill.

Hance, William

1970 *Population, Migration, and Urbanization in Africa.* New
York: Columbia University Press.

Hannerz, Ulf

1969 *Soulside.* New York: Columbia University Press.

Henslin, James
    1968 "Trust and the Cab Driver," in *Sociology and Everyday Life* (ed. M. Truzzi) pp. 138–158. New Jersey: Prentice Hall.

Hughes, Everett C.
    1958 *Men and Their Work.* New York: The Free Press.

Hunter, Guy
    1963 *Education for a Developing Region.* London: George Allen and Unwin Ltd.

Isaacs, K. S., J. M. Alexander, and E. A. Haggard
    1963 "Faith, Trust and Gullibility," *The International Journal of Psycho-Analysis* 44:461–469.

Keller, Suzanne
    1968 *The Urban Neighborhood.* New York: Random House.

Krapf-Askari, Eva
    1969 *Yoruba Towns and Cities.* London: Oxford University Press.

Kumalo, C.
    1966 "African Elites in Industrial Bureaucracy," in *The New Elites of Tropical Africa* (ed. P. C. Lloyd) pp. 216–229. London: Oxford University Press.

Kuper, Leo
    1965 *An African Bourgeoisie.* New Haven: Yale University Press.

Leach, E. R.
    1954 *Political Systems of Highland Burma.* London: G. Bell and Sons, Ltd.

Liebow, Eliot
    1967 *Tally's Corner.* Boston: Little, Brown and Company.

Lloyd, P. C.
  1966 "Introduction," in *The New Elites of Tropical Africa* (ed.
      P. C. Lloyd) pp. 1–65. London: Oxford University Press.
  1967 "The Elite," in *The City of Ibadan* (ed. P. C. Lloyd, A. L.
      Mabogunje, and B. Awe) pp. 129–150. London: Oxford
      University Press.

McCall, George and J. L. Simmons
  1966 *Identities and Interactions.* New York: The Free Press.

Mayer, Philip
  1961 *Townsmen or Tribesmen.* London: Oxford University
      Press.

Milgram, S.
  1967 "The Small World Problem," *Psychology Today* 1: 61–67.

Mitchell, J. Clyde
  1961 "Social Change and the Stability of African Marriages
      in Northern Rhodesia," in *Social Change in Modern
      Africa* (ed. A. Southall) pp. 316–329. London: Oxford
      University Press.
  1969 "The Concept and Use of Social Networks," in *Social
      Networks in Urban Situations* (ed. J. C. Mitchell) pp.
      1–50. New York: Humanities Press, Inc.

Morris, H. S.
  1968 *The Indians in Uganda.* London: Weidenfeld and
      Nicolson.

Nelkin, Dorothy
  1970 "Unpredictability and Life Style in a Migrant Labor
      Camp," *Social Problems* 17:4:472–486.

O'Connor, A. M.
  1965 *Railways and Development in Uganda.* London: Oxford
      University Press.

O'Connor, K. K.
  1962 *Report of the Commission Appointed to Review the Boundary
      Between the Districts of Bugisu and Bukedi.* Entebbe,
      Uganda: Government Printer.

Parkin, David
    1969 *Neighbors and Nationals in an African City Ward.*
        Berkeley and Los Angeles: University of California
        Press.

Pitts, Jesse R.
    1968 "Social Control," in *International Encyclopedia of the Social
        Sciences,* v. 14, pp. 381–396.

Richards, A. I.
    1964 "Authority Patterns in Traditional Buganda," in *The
        King's Men* (ed. L. A. Fallers) pp. 256–293. London:
        Oxford University Press.

Sahlins, M.
    1965 "On the Sociology of Primitive Exchange," in *The
        Relevance of Models for Social Anthropology* (ed. M.
        Banton) pp. 139–236. London: Tavistock Publications
        Ltd.

Schneider, David
    1968 *American Kinship: A Cultural Account.* Englewood Cliffs,
        New Jersey: Prentice-Hall, Inc.

Simmel, G.
    1950 *The Sociology of Georg Simmel.* (trans. and ed. K. H.
        Wolff). New York: The Free Press.

Smythe, Hugh and Mabel M.
    1960 *The New Nigerian Elite.* Stanford: Stanford University
        Press.

Sofer, Cyril and Rhona
    1955 *Jinja Transformed.* Kampala: East African Institute of
        Social Research.

Southall, A. W.
    1966 "The Concept of Elites and their Formation in Uganda,"
        in *The New Elites of Tropical Africa* (ed. P. C. Lloyd) pp.
        342–366. London: Oxford University Press.

Southall, A. W. and P. C. W. Gutkind
    1956 *Townsmen in the Making.* Kampala: East African
        Institute of Social Research.

Suttles, Gerald
 1968 *The Social Order of the Slum.* Chicago: The University of
 Chicago Press.

Travers, J. and S. Milgram
 1969 "An Experimental Study of the Small World Problem,"
 Sociometry 32:425–443.

Turner, V. W.
 1957 *Schism and Continuity in an African Society.* Manchester:
 Manchester University Press.

Twaddle, Michael
 1966 "The Founding of Mbale," in *The Uganda Journal*
 30:1:25–38.

Uganda Government
 1965 *Enumeration of Employees, June 1964.* Entebbe, Uganda:
 Government Press.

Watson, William
 1964 "Social Mobility and Social Class in Industrial
 Communities," in *Closed Systems and Open Minds* (ed.
 M. Gluckman) pp. 129–157. Chicago: Aldine Publishing
 Company.

Whyte, William H. Jr.
 1956 *The Organization Man.* New York: Doubleday and
 Company, Inc.

Wilson, Monica
 1951 *Good Company.* London: Oxford University Press.

Wirth, Louis
 1964 [1938] "Urbanism as a Way of Life," *American Journal of
 Sociology* 44:1–24. Reprinted in *On Cities and Social Life*
 (ed. A. J. Reiss, Jr.) pp. 60–84. Chicago: The University
 of Chicago Press.

Wolf, Eric
 1966 "Kinship, Friendship and Patron-Client Relations in
 Complex Societies," in *The Social Anthropology of*

Complex Societies (ed. M. Banton) pp. 1–20. London: Tavistock Publications Limited.

Wood, M. M.
　1934 *The Stranger: A Study in Social Relationships.* New York: Columbia University Press.

Young, Michael and Peter Wilmott
　1957 *Family and Kinship in East London.* Baltimore: Penguin Books.

Index